Please return to
Clive Nixon.

# Speed Reading Made Easy

## 6 Steps To Reading Excellence

*by Arlyne F. Rial*

DOUBLEDAY & COMPANY, INC.
Garden City, New York
1985

Library of Congress Cataloging in Publication Data

Rial, Arlyne F.
    Speed reading made easy.

    Bibliography: p.
    1. Rapid reading. I. Title.
LB1050.54.R5 1985        428.4'3
ISBN 0-385-19835-3

Photo credits: Nan and Charles Gropman, Arlyne Rial,
Marian Sowell, Marian Mueller, Jeff Ceriani, Libby
Hopkins, Gary Louzon, Ron Thal and Bill Sheperd.
Illustrations by Arlyne Rial.

Library of Congress catalogue number 85-6725

# Speed Reading Made Easy

## 6 Steps To Reading Excellence

*includes:*

*Reading and Speed Reading*

*Comprehension*

*Memory*

*Writing*

*Left and Right Brain Creative Thinking*

*Logical Note-Taking*

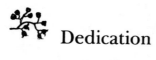 **Dedication**

To my children
Heather, Ricky and Amber
and to my husband, Wayne.

*Special Dedication*

*To World Literacy*

## Knowledge and beauty

*I now want to know*
*all things under the sun,*
*and the moon, too.*

*For all things are beautiful in themselves.*
*and become more beautiful when known to man.*
*Knowledge is life with wings.*

— From Kahlil Gibran

## *Acknowledgements*
### *Most important of all*

Many people made this book eminently more readable and have been enormously helpful in tightening my manuscript during the final drafting. **Dianne Millerbis** and **Carole McCormack** have an unusual sense for what does or does not work on paper. A direct result of the final editing and polishing by **Peyton H. Moss, Jr.** is the glow I now feel wouldn't have been possible without his knowledge and expertise.. **Betty Fereira** kept up with meticulous typing unscrambling early scribblings into something that resembled a book.

**Helene Chalfin** was a major contributor in the original work entitled *Speed Reading Made Easy*. Her extraordinary and matchless care in deciphering and re-writing my scribblings and verbalizations sharpened and polished the text and efforts from the inception.

**Bonnie Blum's** efforts in this revision helped bring clarity and substance to my researched work. Bonnie's spiritual assistance often cheered me on when things looked impossible. **John Wester's** word play and descriptive paragraph on poetry were a nice balancing touch, much appreciated, as were the many hours put in by **Gael Varsi** and **Shirley Schuldt** on the typesetter.

**Charles** and **Nan Gropman** brought light and beauty through their photographs and Charles' help with layout and design, plus the many week-ends devoted to this work, have not gone unnoticed. I want to thank all those who gave of their time in the creation of the photo sections. Among those who contributed to the photo section are: **Marian Sowell**, whose lovely photos are such inspirational statements and add much music to my book, as do the works of **Robbi Drury, Marian Mueller, Lisa** and **Sussanne Helminiak, Ellen** and **Joe Martinez** and **Laura Loesch, Mike Sullivan**, all the **Pyeatt** family, the **Figueiredo** family, **Joe Braga, Jeff Ceriani, Paul Silver** and family, and all the business folks who participated in this project. My gratitude and thanks also go to **Theo Wilner** and little **Autumn** for their warm and wonderful photos.

**Mark Millsaps** and his family were very inspirational and supportive of my efforts as was Mark, who is a truly wonderful student, and along with **Steve Alvarez** and **Susan.** Susan will assist in the bilingual translations in French and Spanish and has encouraged my efforts for several years. A special thank you to **Mary** and **Justin Kendall** for their efforts in helping to promote and to gain acceptance of my ideas.

A very special thank you to **Mendocino Lithographers** and **Philip** and **Grace Sharples** for the expertise, care, space and resources without which the resulting completion would have been impossible. Phil and Grace were also responsible for my first book's completion and offered invaluable help and advice.

Of critical importance was the contribution and input, through these seventeen years, of the many, many teachers, business people and students who clarified my frantic search for facts regarding reading excellence and how to attain it for the good of all.

Most of all, my love and gratitude to my family, my daughters **Heather** and **Amber** and my son **Rick**, plus the efforts of my husband **Wayne**, for understanding me and supporting me all these years so that I could be free to pursue my drives and goals.

My quest for World Literacy could not have continued without their support and love.

## *A note from the author.*

Everything contained here-in has really happened and has been researched for seventeen years by the author.

The methodology used in this course was obtained from the experimentation of reading and memory techniques used by those fortunate individuals we all have envied and admired, known as geniuses and those with photographic minds and those who exceed in school and business and in life.

Men, women and children from all walks of life, and all educational backgrounds were taught the "Rial" *Mechanics of Reading* with success. Many thousands of students were the fertile ground for all the research.

This book is dedicated to all those gentle, wonderous spirits whose thoughts and drives were minutely recorded and their methods preserved on the following pages for all those interested in a natural and useful way to read, comprehend and remember the way the experts do.

**Wondering is just the beginning of intellectual discovery.**

Those persons interviewed and researched, those we call geniuses or super achievers all had shown curiosity and interest in the most tiny details of our universe, such as ants, flowers and sea creatures often ignored.

You will notice, all through this course book, graphics appear of common weeds, common insects and crustaceans. These lowly creatures are most often overlooked because they **are** so common, but, consider this ... when we overlook the minute details of our existence, we become more and more distant from our own intelligence and existence. That is to say, ignoring nature, is in fact, ignoring something very basic within one's own mind and being.

# Table of Contents

# *Foreword*

# The method.

Reading is a natural process. This manual will help you to improve that process, using a series of simple, proven techniques. This natural method of reading will help you to improve your reading skills significantly, whatever your educational attainments or profession.

This manual draws from educational research, scientific studies and theories. I seek to translate this material into a living experience for you. For 17 years, I have guided thousands of students in this natural way to higher quality reading. This work is the synthesis of that teaching, presented in a group of practical techniques.

# This book will train you to concentrate and read:

[1] With a flexibility in purpose, speed, memory notation.

[2] At many times faster than your initial reading rate.

[3] Using your hand, eyes and mind as natural tools for reading.

[4] In groups of words for *ideas*, rather than words one by one.

[5] With a specific purpose in mind, depending on stage of process and type of material.

[6] To increase your memory through the use of effective symbols and special exercises to train both right and left hemispheres of the brain.

# Attainments from this course.

This course will train you how to read faster and with clearer retention and understanding. You will read accounts of some of my students' personal successes, using their new found knowledge of speed reading techniques.

**Imagine reading 200 words per minute and in a short time, increasing your speed to 500 words per minute, or more.**

My *average* student actually reads more rapidly than this. Hard to believe? As the work unfolds, you will see that you don't have to be a genius in order to become a proficient speed reader. In my teaching experience with more than 5,000 men, women and children, there is not one who has not significantly increased **reading speed, memory and comprehension**, with the techniques I will show you.

*First* – I will teach you to test your beginning reading speed on standard and simple materials. I will establish your initial speed, then increase it dramatically by developing a natural reading rhythm you are comfortable using. The reading tempo you set for yourself will depend upon learning to coordinate the functions of your hand, eye and mind. I will teach you **harmony of hand, eye and mind while reading.**

*Second* – I will teach you to **overcome reading regression**, a habit which compels you to re-read parts of passages and paragraphs before you complete the material. You will understand how to stop reading regression when you learn to see words in **groups** as representative of **concepts**, rather than seeing them word for word as single symbols for single ideas. This approach to reading will help you to **understand and**

**remember eighty to ninety percent of everything you read**. I will show you how to concentrate and "key-in" for reading.

*Third* – I will help you to **change your reading behavior**, not only by increasing your ability in area reading but by developing the habit of setting a purpose for yourself before you begin to read. Your decisions about what you read, why you want to read it, and how you will read it will affect your comprehension and memory simultaneously. I will show you how and why **decision making** works for you.

*Fourth* – You will be introduced to scanning and re-scanning; the before and after of actual reading. This helps you *set the purpose* for reading, *anticipate what the material is about* and *obtain a complete mental picture* of the details of the material. Your reading tempo will change, depending on the type of material you are reading.

**Your hand will be the conductor for your eye and mind, setting the right tempo.**

*Fifth* – As you become accustomed to reading for thought instead of word by word, you will begin to understand **peripheral vision and full-dimensional learning**. You will learn to relax to set a focus for your eyes across the page instead of on a tiny portion of the page, and to see words as fast as you can form thoughts. Words will be understood not in themselves but in terms of their association with thoughts.

*Sixth* – You will learn how to develop your memory and store important information through special exercises and the use of **memory mandalas**. These mandalas impress upon you through symbols and key words, the meaning and the relationships of the **who, what,**

**when, where, why** and **how** of a piece. You will become proficient at imaginative note-taking and learn to break up an author's ideas into meaningful, useful patterns that apply personally to you and your purpose in reading. Both left and right hemispheres of the brain will get plenty of exercise using mandalas.

I will show you how to approach different types of reading material, beginning with your favorite newspapers and magazines. You will advance to short stories, depth novels, technical articles and scientific journals. You will explore abstract reports, textbooks, fiction, tests and research papers, pleasure reading and business correspondence.

**From now on, you will read everything for the rest of your life, using proficiently advanced skills.**

I will make you aware of your continued success by having you remeasure your achievement in speed and memory throughout the course.

My course will teach you to be a creative and flexible reader for the rest of your life. The learning process will be a pleasurable and enlightening one.

# To succeed:

You need a true desire and willingness to change your old habits into new and better ones; you must follow the lessons as taught and **practice at least one hour** per day. Follow the directions given **without variation**.

A section for creative and personalized approach to reading memory will be introduced to you when you are taught to use **memory mandalas**. You should keep track of your reading rates, and save the pages where you record information from books – be your own record keeper.

*Remember* – **you must apply these new reading techniques to all of the subsequent reading material you attempt so as to rid yourself of old habits for good. Follow this rule and your progress will be short and simple.**

This program has been developed to improve each person's capacity for self-help. This course will dramatically and permanently increase reading and comprehension. You will be able to read:

1. **A paperback novel in half an hour.**
2. **A magazine article in two or three minutes.**
3. **A textbook chapter in minutes instead of hours.**

You will also be able to:

1. **Remember whole passages with ease.**
2. **Work with purpose and relax.**
3. **Gain a better command of the language.**
4. **Enjoy work-related or entertaining reading materials.**
5. **Learn how to write down and remember notes in a unique and visually stimulating fashion.**

### *Your attitude affects the way you learn*

Through this course, you will learn to break down the barriers you have built up towards your own reading potential. The barriers are of two types:

[1.] **Preconceived emotional attitudes towards your abilities.**

[2.] **Habits which limit both your reading speed and your comprehension.**

This course was designed with **you** in mind. It will show you how to **learn**, how to **remember**, how to **understand** what you read.

This course will show you how easy it is to succeed. Listen, try, and amaze yourself; you have nothing to lose and everything to gain, including a more powerful memory and a deeper understanding of everything you read. Thousands have tried and found this easy, fun and very rewarding. Take total responsibility for your own brain and body. Become the captain of your own ship and set your destination. You will surely reach it if you only have the **desire** to get there.

Try the simple steps and as you learn, watch your attitude change, watch your reading habits change. Each little success is a branch on the learning tree.

## Step I. Reading Preparation

TOMCAT CLOVER

# *Step I*

## *Timing — Sectioning — Underlining*

## A. Finding out how rapidly you read right now.

Try this little test:

**Select** an article or interesting short story and choose a section to read for your initial reading rate, or turn the page and use my selection, "The Bet."

**Read** first in your own way. Time yourself using the second-hand of a watch or clock. Another handy way to time yourself is to use the timer on your stove or range. Or ask a friend or relative to do the initial timing test. Write down how many minutes it took you to read the selection.

Use the chart below to find your present speed or use the pre-calculated chart on page ___ following my selection, "The Bet."

**Count** [1] the number of *lines* in the section you have just read.

[2] the number of *words* in one line.

**Multiply** the number of *lines* by the number of *words*. *This will give you the number of words in the section.*

**Divide** by the number of minutes you have taken to read the section. This will give you the number of words per minute.

There are certain things you must do to prepare yourself for reading.

First of all, you must set aside the time to read. Organize your day so that there is a period when your main purpose is to read. Focus your attention towards this purpose and then begin.

You already know that when you are too tired to read, trying is a waste of time. Don't bother. You also know that in the beginning, it is very important to not have people or distractions around you. Remember, now, you are starting a new thing and you need to be in a place where no one will disturb you for at least an hour each day.

*You owe it to yourself*
*to set this time aside.*
*The world needs you!*

If a friend or relative volunteers to help you to time your first reading, have them stop you every minute. Several one minute readings should give you a good indication of the speed with which you are reading that particular article or story. [Use the chart provided on page 37.]

While your friend or relative is timing you, each sixty second reminder should be recorded by penciling in a mark such as an "×" or "dot" in the margin where you were stopped.

Expect each reading to vary somewhat according to interest or involvement. It is not unusual at first, to read three individual one minute articles at speeds differing by fifty words or more. In other words, if you read for the first minute at two hundred words per minute, you might read the second minute at one hundred and fifty words per minute. Add them together (200 plus 150) and you are reading 350 words every two minutes or divide 350 by two to get your average words per minute, or 175 words per minute. Your speed will differ greatly depending on interest, knowledge, experience, physical condition, and expertise. You will never read steadily at any one given speed, but you can know and should know your average starting speed. That is why I suggest three separate one minute timings.

*Knowing* your average speed (WPM\*) allows you to plan goals for increasing your speed and comprehension. Using the methods provided in this course you can then plan *how* to accomplish these goals. When one sets a goal, arrival at that goal is then possible.

A reasonable goal to start with would be to increase your speed by one hundred words per week. If you use my six steps and practice one hour per day, there is no reason why you cannot accomplish this.

**\*WPM = Words Per Minute**

# Test your reading speed.

**Select** an article or interesting short story.

**Read** first in your old way. Don't underline. Time yourself for one minute.

**Count**:

   [1] the number of *lines* in the section you have just read.

   [2] the number of *words* in one line.

**Multiply** the number of *lines* by the number of *words*. This will give you the number of words in the section.

**Divide** by the number of minutes you have taken to read the section. This will give you the number of words per minute.

## Memory difficulty?

If, after reading my selection, "The Bet," or your selection, you feel you cannot remember all that you would have liked to remember, such as the main idea or characters, or any of the other important ideas about the story then, my suggestion to you, dear student, is to turn to **Step V**, entitled **Decisions & Memory**, starting on page 163.

The easy and ready-to-use techniques and memory builders will fortify all your subsequent readings.

Refer often to **Step V** by clipping a colored plastic tag or other identifying mark to the edge of the first page of that chapter, or use a bookmark.

# The Bet

## ANTON CHEKHOV

It was a dark autumn night. The old banker was pacing from corner to corner of his study, recalling to his mind the party he gave in the autumn fifteen years before. There were many clever people at the party and much interesting conversation. They talked among other things of capital punishment. The guests, among them not a few scholars and journalists, for the most part disapproved of capital punishment. They found it obsolete as a means of punishment, unfitted to a Christian State and immoral. Some of them thought that capital punishment should be replaced universally by life-imprisonment.

**100**

"I don't agree with you," said the host. "I myself have experienced neither capital punishment nor life-imprisonment, but if one may judge *a priori,* then in my opinion capital punishment is more moral and more humane than imprisonment. Execution kills instantly, life-imprisonment kills by degrees. Who is the more humane executioner, one who kills you in a few seconds or one who draws the life out of you incessantly, for years?"

"They're both equally immoral," remarked one of the guests, "because their purpose is the same, to take away life. The State is not God. It has no right to take away that which it cannot give back, if it should so desire."

**200**

Among the company was a lawyer, a young man of about twenty-five. On being asked his opinion, he said:

"Capital punishment and life-imprisonment are equally immoral; but if I were offered the choice between them, I would certainly choose the second. It's better to live somehow than not to live at all."

There ensued a lively discussion. The banker, who was then younger and more nervous, suddenly lost his temper, banged his fist on the table, and turning to the young lawyer, cried out:

**300**

"It's a lie. I bet you two millions you wouldn't stick in a cell even for five years."

"If you mean it seriously," replied the lawyer, "then I bet I'll stay not five but fifteen."

"Fifteen! Done!" cried the banker. "Gentlemen, I stake two millions."

400    "Agreed. You stake two millions, I my freedom," said the lawyer.

So this wild, ridiculous bet came to pass. The banker, who at that time had too many millions to count, spoiled and capricious, was beside himself with rapture. During supper he said to the lawyer jokingly:

"Come to your senses, young man, before it's too late. Two millions are nothing to me, but you stand to lose three or four of the best years of your life. I say three or four, because you'll never stick it out any longer. Don't forget either, you unhappy man, that voluntary is much

500    heavier than enforced imprisonment. The idea that you have the right to free yourself at any moment will poison the whole of your life in the cell. I pity you."

And now the banker, pacing from corner to corner, recalled all this and asked himself:

"Why did I make this bet? What's the good? The lawyer loses fifteen years of his life and I throw away two millions. Will it convince people that capital punishment is worse or better than imprisonment for life? No, no! all stuff and rubbish. On my part, it was a caprice of a

600    well-fed man; on the lawyer's pure greed of gold."

He recollected further what happened after the evening party. It was decided that the lawyer must undergo his imprisonment under the strictest observation, in a garden wing of the banker's house. It was agreed that during the period he would be deprived of the right to cross the threshold, to see living people, to hear human voices, and to receive letters and newspapers. He was permitted to have a musical instrument, to read books, to write letters, to drink wine and smoke tobacco. By the agreement he could

700    communicate, but only in silence, with the outside world through a little window specially constructed for this purpose. Everything necessary, books, music, wine, he could receive in any quantity by sending a note through the window. The agreement provided for all the minutest details, which made the confinement strictly solitary, and it obliged the lawyer to remain exactly fifteen years from twelve o'clock of November 14th, 1870, to twelve o'clock of November 14th, 1885. The

least attempt on his part to violate the time, freed the banker from the obligation to pay him the two millions. **800**

During the first year of imprisonment, the lawyer, as far as it was possible to judge from his short notes, suffered terribly from loneliness and boredom. From his wing day and night came the sound of the piano. He rejected wine and tobacco. "Wine," he wrote, "excites desires, and desires are the chief foes of a prisoner; besides, nothing is more boring than to drink good wine alone, and tobacco spoils the air in his room." During the first year the lawyer was sent books of a light character; novels with a complicated love interest, stories of crime **900** and fantasy, comedies, and so on.

In the second year the piano was heard no longer and the lawyer asked only for classics. In the fifth year, music was heard again, and the prisoner asked for wine. Those who watched him said that during the whole of that year he was only eating, drinking, and lying on his bed. He yawned often and talked angrily to himself. Books he did not read. Sometimes at night he would sit down to write. He would write for a long time and tear it all up in the **1000** morning. More than once he was heard to weep.

In the second half of the sixth year, the prisoner began zealously to study languages, philosophy, and history. He fell on these subjects so hungrily that the banker hardly had time to get books enough for him. In the space of four years about six hundred volumes were bought at his request. It was while that passion lasted that the banker received the following letter from the prisoner: "My dear gaoler, I am writing these lines in six languages. Show them to experts. Let them read them. If they do not find **1100** one single mistake, I beg you to give orders to have a gun fired off in the garden. By the noise I shall know that my efforts have not been in vain. The geniuses of all ages and countries speak in different languages; but in them all burns the same flame. Oh, if you knew my heavenly happiness now that I can understand them!" The prisoner's desire was fulfilled. Two shots were fired in the garden by the banker's order.

Later on, after the tenth year, the lawyer sat immovable before his table and read only the New **1200** Testament. The banker found it strange that a man who in four years had mastered six hundred erudite volumes, should have spent nearly a year in reading one book, easy to understand and by no means thick. The

New Testament was then replaced by the history of religions and theology.

During the last two years of his confinement the prisoner read an extraordinary amount, quite haphazard. Now he would apply himself to the natural sciences, then he would read Byron or Shakespeare. Notes used to come from him in which he asked to be sent at the same time a book on chemistry, a textbook of medicine, a novel, and some treatise on philosophy or theology. He read as though he were swimming in the sea among broken pieces of wreckage, and in his desire to save his life was eagerly grasping one piece after another.

## II

The banker recalled all this, and thought:

"Tomorrow at twelve o'clock he receives his freedom. Under the agreement, I shall have to pay him two millions. If I pay, it's all over with me; I am ruined forever..."

Fifteen years before he had too many millions to count, but now he was afraid to ask himself which he had more of, money or debts. Gambling on the Stock-Exchange, risky speculation, and the recklessness of which he could not rid himself even in old age, had gradually brought his business to decay; and the fearless, self-confident, proud man of business had become an ordinary banker, trembling at every rise and fall in the market.

"That cursed bet," murmured the old man clutching his head in despair.... "Why didn't the man die? He's only forty years old. He will take away my last farthing, marry, enjoy life, gamble on the Exchange, and I will look on like an envious beggar and hear the same words from him every day: 'I'm obliged to you for the happiness of my life. Let me help you.' No, it's too much! The only escape from bankruptcy and disgrace — is that the man should die."

The clock had just struck three. The banker was listening. In the house every one was asleep, and one could hear only the frozen trees whining outside the windows. Trying to make no sound, he took out of his safe the key of the door which had not been opened for fifteen years, put on his overcoat, and went out of the house. The garden was dark and cold. It was raining. A damp, penetrating wind howled in the garden and gave the trees no rest. Though he strained his eyes, the banker could see neither the ground, nor the white statues, nor the garden wing, nor the trees. Approaching the garden wing, he called the watchman twice. There was no answer. Evidently the watchman had taken shelter from the bad weather and was now asleep somewhere in the kitchen or the greenhouse.

1700

"If I have the courage to fulfill my intention," thought the old man, "the suspicion will fall on the watchman first of all."

In the darkness he groped for the steps and the door and entered the hall of the garden-wing, then poked his way into a narrow passage and struck a match. Not a soul was there. Someone's bed, with no bedclothes on it, stood there, and an iron stove loomed dark in the corner. The seals on the door that led into the prisoner's room were unbroken.

1800

When the match went out, the old man, trembling from agitation, peeped into the little window.

In the prisoner's room a candle was burning dimly. The prisoner himself sat by the table. Only his back, the hair on his head and his hands were visible. Open books were strewn about on the table, the two chairs, and on the carpet near the table.

Five minutes passed and the prisoner never once stirred. Fifteen years' confinement had taught him to sit motionless. The banker tapped on the window with his finger, but the prisoner made no movement in reply. Then the banker cautiously tore the seals from the door and put the key into the lock. The rusty lock gave a hoarse groan and the door creaked. The banker expected instantly to hear a cry of surprise and the sound of steps. Three minutes passed and it was as quiet as it had been before. He made up his mind to enter.

1900

Before the table sat a man, unlike an ordinary human being. It was a skeleton, with tight-drawn skin, with long curly hair like a woman's, and a shaggy beard. The color of his face was yellow, of an earthy shade; the cheeks were sunken, the back long and narrow, and the hand upon which he leaned his hairy head was so lean and skinny that it was painful to look upon. His hair was already silvering with gray, and no one who glanced at the senile emaciation of the face would have believed

2000

that he was only forty years old. On the table, before his bended head, lay a sheet of paper on which something was written in a tiny hand.

"Poor devil," thought the banker, "he's asleep and probably seeing millions in his dreams. I have only to take and throw this half-dead thing on the bed, smother him a moment with the pillow, and the most careful examination will find no trace of unnatural death. but, first, let us read what he has written here."

The banker took the sheet from the table and read:

"Tomorrow at twelve o'clock midnight, I shall obtain my freedom and the right to mix with people. But before I leave this room and see the sun I think it necessary to say a few words to you. On my own clear conscience and before God who sees me I declare to you that I despise freedom, life, health, and all that your books call the blessings of the world.

"For fifteen years I have diligently studied earthly life. True, I saw neither the earth nor the people, but in your books I drank fragrant wine, sang songs, hunted deer and wild boar in the forests, loved women. . . . And beautiful women, like clouds ethereal, created by the magic of your poets' genius, visited me by night and whispered to me wonderful tales, which made my head drunken. In your books I climbed the summits of Elburz and Mont Blanc and saw from there how the sun rose in the morning, and in the evening suffused the sky, the ocean, and the mountain ridges with a purple gold. I saw from there how above me lightning glimmered cleaving the clouds; I saw green forests, fields, rivers, lakes cities; I heard sirens singing, and the playing of the pipes of Pan; I touched the wings of beautiful devils who came flying to me to speak of God. . . . In your books I cast myself into bottomless abysses, worked miracles, burned cities to the ground, preached new religions, conquered whole countries. . . .

"Your books gave me wisdom. All that unwearying human thought created in the centuries is compressed to a little lump in my skull. I know that I am cleverer than you all.

"And I despise your books, despise all worldly blessings and wisdom. Everything is void, frail, visionary and delusive as a mirage. Though you be proud and wise and beautiful, yet will death wipe you from the face of the earth like the mice underground; and your posterity,

36

your history, and the immortality of your men of genius will be as frozen slag, burnt down together with the terrestial globe.

"You are mad, and gone the wrong way. You take falsehood for truth and ugliness for beauty. You would marvel if suddenly apple and orange trees should bear frogs and lizards instead of fruit, and if roses should begin to breathe the odor of a sweating horse. So do I marvel at you, who have bartered heaven for earth. I do not want to understand you.   **2600**

"That I may show you in deed my contempt for that by which you live, I waive the two millions of which I once dreamed of as paradise, and which I now despise. That I may deprive myself of my right to them, I shall come out from here five minutes before the stipulated term, and thus shall violate the agreement."

When he had read, the banker put the sheet on the table, kissed the head of the strange man, and began to weep. He went out of the wing. Never at any other time,   **2700** not even after his terrible losses on the Exchange, had he felt such contempt for himself as now. Coming home, he lay down on his bed, but agitation and tears kept him a long time from sleeping. . . . . .

The next morning the poor watchman came running to him and told him that they had seen the man who lived in the wing climb through the window into the garden. He had gone to the gate and disappeared. The banker instantly went with his servants to the wing and established the escape of his prisoner. To avoid   **2800** unnecessary rumors he took the paper with the renunciation from the table, and, on his return, locked it in his safe.   **2820**

## Original Words Per Minute
## OWPM

To find your reading rate, count the elapsed reading time to the nearest number of minutes and ¼ minutes (e.g. 1 minute and 16 seconds would equal 1.25 on the rate chart). In this way you can calculate your **OWPM**.

| 1,000 WORDS | | 2,000 WORDS | | 3,000 WORDS | |
|---|---|---|---|---|---|
| Minutes | WPM | Minutes | WPM | Minutes | WPM |
| .25 | 4,000 | .25 | 8,000 | .25 | 12,000 |
| .50 | 2,000 | .50 | 4,000 | .50 | 6,000 |
| .75 | 1,333 | .75 | 2,666 | .75 | 3999 |
| 1.00 | 1,000 | 1.00 | 2,000 | 1.00 | 3,000 |
| 1.25 | 800 | 1.25 | 1,600 | 1.25 | 2,400 |
| 1.50 | 666 | 1.50 | 1,332 | 1.50 | 1,998 |
| 1.75 | 571 | 1.75 | 1,142 | 1.75 | 1,713 |
| 2.00 | 500 | 2.00 | 1,000 | 2.00 | 1,500 |

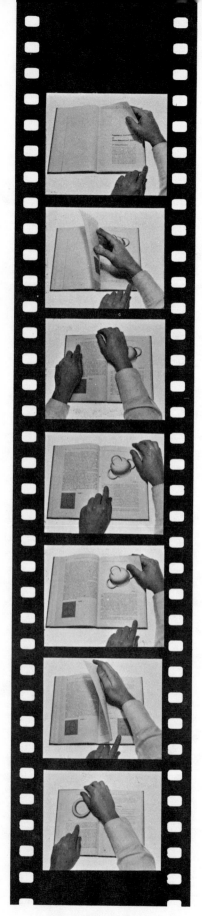

left-handed

## B. How to hold your reading material.

It is important to hold your book properly while reading, in order to avoid fatigue. Have you often found yourself falling asleep while studying? Have you then tried to go to bed and not been able to fall asleep because you feel guilty about all the unfinished reading you were expected to complete? Don't feel too badly. This is not unusual, and has happened to most of us at one time or another.

Why do you feel fatigue?

When you try to read with your book at an uneven angle, you will inadvertently place unnecessary strain on your shoulders and back. After ten minutes or so, your body will begin to send you 'messages.' You might start to fidget, or feel a painful sensation in your neck or shoulders, get a tension headache, or, like so many people, just get downright sleepy. Have any of these things ever happened to you while you were reading? If so, I have some **good** news for you. To avoid fatigue, strain and tension while reading, you need only start with this simple rule:

**From this day forth, hold your reading material as pictured, and keep your feet flat on the floor. Sit in as straight a position as possible, thus avoiding stress on your vertebrae.**

# Another easy tip:

Before you start, **break in the book**. Flip through the pages, making the book comfortable to work with. Ruffle the corners first. Now you must think about effectively positioning your hands before you can even start to turn the pages. If you are right handed, your left hand turns, right hand underlines; if you are left handed, the opposite is true.

## NEVER – NEVER – NEVER

1. **Read without holding your book properly**
2. **Read without sectioning off pages with rubberbands or paper clips.** [See next page.]
3. **Read without purpose — knowing the reasons for reading the selection.**

## WHEN YOU PRACTICE:

Use only enjoyable materials for your first practice sessions. Practice **only** on easily read articles. Use newspapers, magazines, pamphlets, easy short stories. Just remember to practice **every day.** Out of the twenty four hours in each day, I'm sure you can find one hour for your very own improvement. Remember, the world needs you.

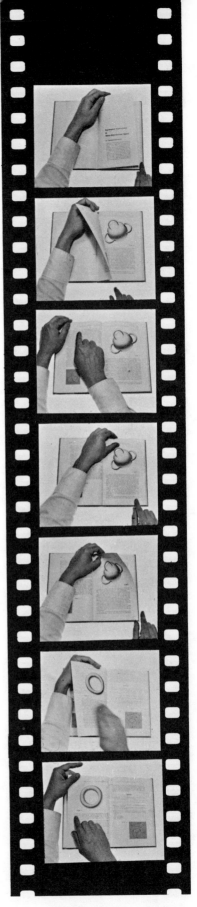

right-handed

# Ridding yourself of some mental hang-ups.

## Rubberbands and Paper Clips

Most people will be wary of a book six or seven hundred pages long. They silently say to themselves, "Why buy that book? I'd never finish it even if I did start it." Other people, however, will buy a book just to impress their friends. After all, it is a prestigious feeling when friends come to visit your house and see many currently popular books on the shelves. Some people I know have home libraries filled with famous, best-selling books. When I ask them if they have read these books, they often reply, "No, but someday I will." After years of probing questions, I have found that the main reason people do not start books is the length of a volume alone. A thick book will scare away many a reader.

There is a very simple solution to this problem. It is called **sectioning.**

First, you read the titles and covers of your books, then begin with Chapter 1, proceeding as follows:

(A) **Separate the chapter from the rest of the volume.** (*See picture*). Then, when you read, read as though each chapter is a 'book' in itself. Always section off chapters with rubberbands. Each chapter is, of course, much smaller in volume than the book, and you will be less likely to be discouraged at the length of one chapter alone. "By the inch, it's a cinch; by the mile, it's a trial."

(B) **Use paper clips to section off magazine articles.** (*See picture on next page*).

# How to "key-in."

**Getting in the mood for a good book**

The first step is to pick up the material at hand. **Handle** the book or magazine; let your sense of touch and sight familiarize you with the material. Look at the cover, title page, table of contents, the front and back flaps. Check pictures and maps and graphs, just with a general glance.

Ask yourself what you already know about this subject: from other books, from conversations, from television or classes. This is a sure way of bringing your concentration to attention.

The next step is to ask yourself "What am I going to do with this information? How will I use it? What will it mean to me?"

Again, flip through the pages, look at the pictures, maps, diagrams and glance at the contents. **Think** about what the author is trying to tell you. Make mental notes on these preliminary conclusions. At this point, your interest and attention should be focused on the reading material in your hands.

*Unless people are trained to* **KEY-IN** and given time and space to do so, their level of *concentration is just left to chance*. Clear thinking is lost.

Each step is a lesson in the mechanics of learning to learn. Become comfortable with each lesson before attempting to go on to the next step. If you are completely ready for each new dimension of the process, you will become a very strong and confident speed reader.

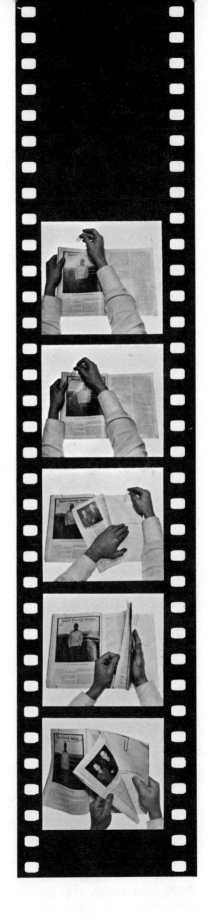

# C. How the experts do it.

Now that you have learned how to time yourself, to hold a book and to organize your practice time, it's time to learn how the experts read.

**Follow this simple rule:**

**Using your hand**, begin with the title and then **"underline"** it.

Next, continue down the page, "underlining" each and every line until you reach the end of the article.

Using your fingers to underline is **necessary** if you ever want to read with any speed.

Follow your fingers. You will amaze yourself with the ease with which you can read and learn. You will never again say that you must read and then re-read in order to understand.

As we underline, our eyes are forced to move along the line of print. Eyes follow moving objects: the hand in motion down the page attracts the eyes to follow. This also provides a **focal point** which aids concentration.

Choose a simple book or magazine article for practice.

[See photo strip on next page.]

**Most of the naturally fast readers interviewed use their hands or fingers when reading.**

# Harmony of eye, hand and mind.

When **using the hand** while reading, we promote what we call full-dimensional reading. The eyes are actually capable of taking in whole areas of print at one time. You can "see" words as fast as you can "think" them, not as fast as you can "say" them. When you "say" a word with your inner mind while you read, it's called "sub-vocalizing". This "hearing" problem slows most readers down to one word at a time. We call this one-dimensional reading. Yet human beings are physiologically capable of seeing and registering **several** words at once. Reading visually from eye to brain contact alone is getting meaning from the words without that "inner voice" that slows you down. As your hand brushes across the page, it helps order your thoughts quickly into consciousness, smoothly and rhythmically. One sweeping glance absorbs several words at one time, bypassing the hearing response. This is how you set your reading tempo. This is how you establish harmony of eye, hand and mind while reading.

The eye can take in more than one word at a time. The eye takes in the book, the page, the table, the room, the light fixtures. In fact, the whole body is a sensor, taking in sounds, sights and sensations such as a chill in the room, or the light reflections on a wall.

The hand as a tool of reading is a tool of the mind. In speed reading, the hand sets the tempo and guides the eyes across the thoughts. It acts as an extension of the mind which helps complete the circuit of thought.

*Start now*, reading the rest of this book using underlining. Soon it will not feel so awkward.

This single change in a short while will totally change your reading speed.

## D. How the experts and naturally fast readers think.

# Knowledge

"Knowledge is power," wrote Francis Bacon in the seventeenth century, at the beginning of the Age of Science. A lack of knowledge is a lack of power and is often responsible for a lack of confidence. If you are missing any of these in your life, you are more likely to fail in school or business, or to drop out of a course, abandon a hobby or be passed up for a promotion at your job. Speed reading can make more knowledge available to you through the use of books. "But," some people have said to me, "people who live in a world of books miss out on the experience of real life."

Two intriguing recent books, Alvin Toffler's *Future Shock* and *The Shape of Minds to Come* by John G. Taylor will tell you how human beings have obtained dominion over all other living forms on earth today due to their ability to **read and write**. They will show you why **the more intelligent an animal is, the better it survives**. They will demonstrate the **growing accumulation of knowledge** in the world today, and how that means **accelerating change in all of our lives**.

**is power**

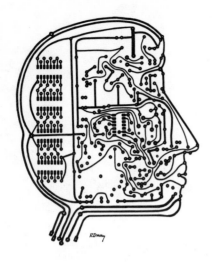

# Brain power.

If you think you are using all of your brain power, then think again. Experts have proven that humans use only a small proportion of their brains and only a small percentage of their mental potential.

For more than a hundred years, scientists have been experimenting to discover the mysteries of the brain and its functioning. One experiment a few years ago at Stanford University tested and measured the powers of damaged brains in rats. A rat placed in a complex maze was rewarded with food each time he could pass through. A portion of the animal's brain was removed and then he was placed in the maze again. He taught himself how to find a way through the maze again to obtain the food. The process was repeated until only a tiny portion of the rat's brain was left. Each time, the rat relearned how to get through the maze.

One meaning of this experiment to me is that we can **retrain our brains** to do anything we **want** or **need** to do. Eye problems and physical handicaps can be overcome by retraining the mind and body to respond to the stimuli. It is a matter of will. If you have enough desire to do something, **it can be done**. Another is that even a damaged brain can do a great deal. In a sense, our brains have been damaged by narrow habits and attitudes. Speed reading helps repair that damage, opening up new horizons of knowledge and adventure.

I met a set of twins in Sacramento about ten years ago who had been told that they had a very rare blood disease and had only two years left to live. One of the boys believed the doctors'

*We have seen evidence of latent superflexibility, 'doing wonders' in adversity on every level. Some examples: the restoration of locomotive patterns in mutilated insects and rats; the emergency redistribution of labor in the beehive ...*

*A rat with its optical cortex cut out can still be taught and retaught the same skills on perception.*

*— THE ACT OF CREATION*
*By Arthur Koestler*

diagnosis and became frantic. In two years he died. The other brother would not accept the doctors' judgment. He took up swimming, skiing and jogging. He outlived the deadline by many years. **We can control our minds and bodies by the power of our own will.**

# Attitude or aptitude?

*Because of this course, one big change will be in your thinking and in the realization of your own abilities.*

IQ tests have definite limitations. Don't spend the rest of your life thinking you are only average or below average in intelligence if you did poorly on such a test when you were young. Expect only the best of yourself. Feel good about yourself. Never put yourself down because of something someone else has said to you. Be kind to yourself and give yourself a fighting chance in any and all ways to improve your mind and body. It has been proven that we **all** use only a limited portion of our brains. Remember that our potential mental energy is as yet undiscovered. Don't set preconceived limitations on your abilities.

Forget the IQ test and remember to *believe in yourself*. A test of IQ is only *one* measure of intelligence and in fact has been subject to question and re-evaluation. Think, rather of the **unlimited mental potential** in each and every human.

Our schools commit the sin of omission; it is what they *don't* do that can be criticized. There is not enough stress on what the person **is** capable of achieving, with positive feedback. In our overcrowded classrooms, with the use of sometimes outmoded texts, and an emphasis on tests for IQ, many students become blind to their own real potential. They turn off to school, become bored, are unable to see their own special abilities and are unwilling even to try to learn. Here is where many of the real emotional blocks to learning begin.

*In the technological systems of tomorrow – fast, fluid and self-regulating – machines will deal with the flow of physical materials; men with the flow of information and insight.*
— FUTURE SHOCK
By Alvin Toffler

**This program has been developed to improve each person's capacity for self-help to increase dramatically and permanently reading and comprehension in a relatively short time.**

# A helpful hint.

I was told as a child that if you paint or sew, or have some hobby, you should always have your tools **handy**. One of my favorite hobbies in painting in oil. Through the years, I've noticed that when my paints and canvases are handy, I seem to turn out more paintings. On the other hand, when I neatly put all of my tools in their little special places, they are truly "out of sight, out of mind" for me.

My helpful hint for you, dear readers, is to always carry some reading material with you wherever you go. Have some handy reading in all the places you are frequently found — your bedroom, bathroom, coffee place, or car — or always carry something to read in your briefcase or purse. All those moments when you have time to spare can be taken up with some reading. This will cut down on boredom as well as allowing you to learn something new , at the same time that you are strengthening your newly acquired speed reading skills. Keep something handy at all times! And remember, **underline everything!** Brochures, magazines, news items, everything. All you need is your hand, and a clear open mind.

*Unlike the flowers of the field, people have much control over their destinies. The flowers are fixed in their environment, while we have the freedom to change our destiny.*

THISTLE POPPY

The science of cybernetics tells us that man has and uses a machine, not that he is a machine. It sees the subconscious mind as not a mind at all but a mechanism — a goal striving servo-mechanism consisting of the brain and nervous system which is used by and directed by the mind.

This mechanism within us is impersonal and automatic. Like any other servo-mechanism, it makes use of stored information or "memory" and it works upon the data we feed into it (our thoughts, beliefs, interpretations). Through our attitudes and interpretations of situations we "describe" the problem to be worked upon. If we feed data in to the effect that we ourselves are unworthy, inferior, undeserving or incapable (a negative self-image) this data, too, is processed and acted upon in solving current problems and responding to current situations. Thus our internal mechanism will work automatically to achieve goals of success and happiness, or unhappiness and failure, depending on the goals which we ourselves set for it.

— YOUR BUILT-IN SUCCESS MECHANISM
By Maxwell Maltz

*Some People Read Simply for the Love of It . . .*

*. . . to keep abreast on the job*

*. . . for the wonder of it*

. . . to keep up

*. . . a diploma worth having*

. . . *for acceptance on the team*

. . . to be informed

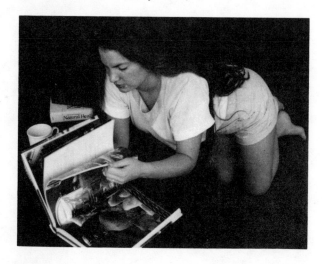

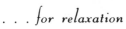

*. . . for relaxation*

*. . . in the hustle and bustle of school*

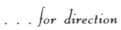

. . . for direction

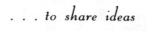

. . . to share ideas

62

*. . . at work*

*. . . for relaxation*

*. . . for sheer joy*

*. . . to expand her expectations*

# Scanning

LITTLE YELLOW SORREL

# *Step II*

## *Scanning — Two Hand Motions*
## *Phase I — Phase II*

# Scanning.

The concept I am introducing is called **SCANNING.**

Scanning is a way of becoming familiar with the **reading territory** before you actually read. After a little practice the scanning process will become so automatic it will be second nature to you.

Imagine that a friend is taking you for a walk to a new place. The path you are following is unfamiliar to you and leads down and around to a beautiful waterfall. Your friend, who has been here many times, skips rapidly around the mountain path, although it is slippery with rain. Yet you step cautiously behind, afraid of every step. Why is your friend so far ahead? Is she/he a better hiker than you or does she/he have more stamina? Both times, of course, the answer is "no." The real reason your friend is ahead is that she/he has **been here before** and has knowledge of the territory, making it familiar.

If you scan over the territory of a book before actually reading, then reading will be easier, just as a path on a mountainside would be easier to walk on if you were already familiar with your destination.

*Scanning involves a new hand motion. Scanning hand motions are large, circular movements covering whole pages in seconds.*

*On the next few pages, you will see diagrams. Study them carefully until the **METHOD** of scanning makes total sense.*

*Three hundred and fifty years after his death, scientists are still finding evidence to support Cervantes' succinct insight into adaptational psychology: To be forewarned is to be forearmed. Self-evident as it may seem, in most situations we can help individuals adapt better if we simply provide them with advance information about what lies ahead.*

*Studies of the reactions of astronauts, displaced families and industrial workers almost uniformly point to this conclusion. Whether the problem is that of driving a car down a crowded street, piloting a plane, solving intellectual puzzles, playing a cello or dealing with interpersonal difficulties, performance improves when the individual knows what to expect next.*

*The mental processing of advance data about any subject, presumably cuts down on the amount of processing and the reaction time during the actual period of adaptation. It was Freud, I believe, who said: "Thought is action in rehearsal."*

— FUTURE SHOCK
By Alvin Toffler

**SCANNING** is a ten-second-per-page preview of reading material. You can use either a "Christmas Tree" hand motion called "The Quest", or you may prefer the "circular" hand motion (whichever is more comfortable). It's up to you. You skip details and simply become familiar with the reading **territory**. This is the purpose of scanning. It allows you to anticipate your material, get a general idea of its tone and content. The more familiar you become with the material, the more quickly and easily you can understand it. As you scan, you ask yourself questions — you know what you are looking for, you know what you want to remember. This is reading with purpose. **Being selective** about what you want from your reading **increases** your reading efficiency. As you ask questions about what you need to learn from the material and what you will do with the information later on, you influence your perception of the input of the words passing from your eye to your brain. What you need to find will seem to stand out from the rest of the writing. Your decisions in reading help to strip away what is irrelevant to your purpose, as the words pass by under your fingers.

You might ask, "But what if the words pass by without registering meaning in my head?" Then find the words that do register. See a whole sentence as a context for a whole thought. See your words always in the context of the sentences, constantly searching for the WHO, WHAT, WHERE, WHEN, WHY and the HOW of it.

*The learning process seems to depend mainly on visual exploration. . . . We finger over the visual field with our gaze . . . The eye may be a camera, but immediately behind its lens there is a series of compensating, correcting, and retouching devices — the perceptual matrices of skilled vision.*

— THE ACT OF CREATION
By Arthur Koestler

*Reading with purpose means searching for answers*

**?**

**WhoWhat
Where
WhenWhy
How**

# TWO BASIC WAYS
# No. 1—Circular

There are two hand motions that you can use in the scanning process. The first is Circular. You will move your hand as follows, at **ten seconds** per page, sweeping down the lines at a fairly fast pace. Ten seconds per page to start. Remember, you are not trying to memorize here. Just trying to *familiarize* yourself with the style and content of each page.

[Study carefully.]

# No. 2—The Quest
### or "Christmas Tree"

Or, if you prefer, you can use the following hand motion down the page: but only ten seconds per page.

[Study carefully.]

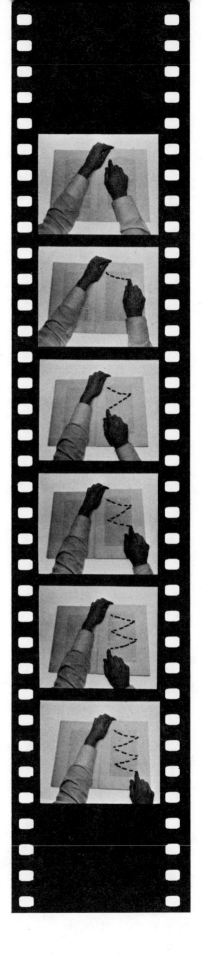

SCARLET LARKSPUR
Delphinium nudicaule

Whichever hand motion you choose, remember, you are **not reading, just scanning**. Use either of these motions for only ten seconds for each page. As you scan, keep in mind the fact that you are searching for information. The more you find now the **faster** you will be able to **read, comprehend, remember**. Also, the more familiar you are with the "territory" of each book, the more you will enjoy reading. *And we all know that we get a lot more out of articles we enjoy!* Keep your hand flowing rapidly down every page until you reach the end of the article or section. The purpose of scanning is to become familiar quickly with the material, so that when you go back to actually read you not only have some idea of the general range it covers, but also **how** you want to read it and what you think you can get from it.

*Before practicing scanning, please read on for fuller explanations.*

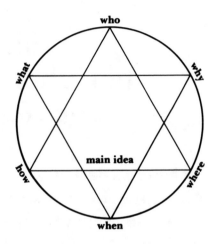

**Star Mandala**
**[See filled in mandalas on pages 108, 115 and 121.]**

# Training peripheral vision for reading.

**Sit before a desk.** Look directly at an object before you — a book or newspaper. Now, **close your eyes.** What else was in your actual range of vision? Name some objects you saw. Now, **look around again**, circling your eyes around the desk. Actually, you can see past the desk, into the room beyond, out the window to the left side, out the door to the right, for example. You can see colors, objects, shapes, and patterns on **all sides** of your point of focus. You can close your eyes and remember which things you have seen. Practice this exercise in different places — indoors, outdoors, in a class, at the store. Your vision will expand as you practice each day and take mental notes on what you see. **Remove those imaginary blinders from your eyes!**

**Learning and using underlining is so natural that there is no reason or way to forget.**

# Peripheral vision and books; full-dimensional reading.

On the printed page, your eyes can take in much more than the word-by-word, line-by-line reading method allows. To gain **reading use** of your peripheral vision, first practice by holding the page a distance from your eyes.

Take in the whole page with your eyes. Many words are falling within your range of vision. You can "catch" some of them without zeroing in on only one line; you can sweep the page and see all the words it contains. This is an introduction to full-dimensional reading. You are obtaining use of your peripheral vision while reading.

Close your eyes and say aloud some of the words you have seen in your quick scan of the page.

Open your eyes and try to absorb the page again, from a distance. Then, close your eyes and remember as many words as you can.

The more you repeat this exercise, the more you will understand how to use your peripheral vision while you read. Expect yourself to be startled by your increase in reading speed after you have removed the blinders to your reading range which most people wear when looking at printed material.

**Remember to use underlining on *all* reading materials.**

# One-dimensional versus full-dimensional reading.

When you see a clock, when you study a painting, it is the **whole** thing that you see, the sum of all the parts. When you read a word, it is the **whole** word you read, not each letter separately. This is the way we want you to read — look for **groups of words** which express ideas. The meaning of what you read is grasped more fully and more quickly when you look at larger groups of words all together. Words are symbols for things we know. When looking at words one at a time, separately, the meaning registered in our brains is incomplete. We must see words **in relationship to one another** in order to comprehend **fully** what we are reading. The faster your rate of sweeping your hand and eyes across the page, the more words you are taking in at one glance. So you are registering **concepts** in speed reading; you are seeing each word in relationship to the others around it. This gives you a more accurate understanding of each word's significance. You understand the full meaning when you see all the words; you only understand the individual symbol when you look at one word at a time. Word-by-word reading is one-dimensional. Reading groups of words is full-dimensional reading.

# Review of underlining and full-dimensional reading.

Now that you have learned about your **natural peripheral reading vision**, it is time to go back to our first step, **underlining, and use them both together.**

**As you learned earlier in the book, your eye follows a moving object, and your hand is a natural underlining tool. You know that the motion of your hand as it underlines each sentence down the page trains your eyes to follow, smoothly and rhythmically, through the complete article. Your eyes are drawn forward. There's little chance of reading in reverse** when you underline with your hand. The inefficient habit of reading regression forces you to read a sentence or paragraph, then go back and read many of the same words over again.

Many people believe that they must re-read sections of material because they cannot remember or understand what they have just read. But when you read in reverse, your mind is going nowhere. The ideas become jumbled, the logical train of thought becomes interrupted and your concentration then dwindles. Also, your reading speed is quite slow if you have no moving hand for your eyes to follow, to set your reading tempo down a page of words. Using your new habit of underlining will correct these reading problems, increasing your speed in such a short time that you actually will have difficulty believing that it is possible. *This new visual tool, coupled with underlining, will aid memory and speed.*

**Remember:**

When you drive, walk, wash dishes, skate, build, or use tools, you are automatically using your peripheral vision. Reading is the *only* activity in which people seem to turn off their natural peripheral vision. They have been taught to read incorrectly. Underlining will change all that for you. Exercises in peripheral vision, using printed matter, or simply viewing a room, a landscape, a painting, all, will help you to **remember your natural ability** to see objects on all sides of your main area of focus. Change your reading style from a one-dimensional habit to full-dimensional enjoyment. Learn to use your natural peripheral reading vision. Open up your eyes! **You can see whole sentences and paragraphs at one time.**

**It's all just a matter of practice and time. The *more time* you put into developing this visual skill, the more competent a reader and thinker you will become. (*Effort has always been rewarded with gain.*)**

**Remember to use underlining on *all* reading materials.**

*PEOPLE TEND TO*
*REMEMBER:*

* *WHAT IS PLEASANT*

* *SIMPLE PATTERNS*

* *VIVID DETAILS*

* *VISUALLY STRIKING MATERIAL*

* *WHAT IS PERSONALLY*
*RELEVANT TO THEM*

* *MATERIAL WHICH HAS*
*BEEN "PROCESSED"*
*— disassembled and reassembled*
*in various ways in their minds.*

* *MATERIAL IN WHICH THEY ARE*
*INTERESTED NOT ONLY AS A WHOLE,*
*BUT ALSO IN TERMS OF ITS DETAILS*

* *FIGURES WITH GOOD CONTOURS*
*WITHIN A "TENSION SYSTEM" FOR RECALL.*

* *MATERIAL TOWARDS WHICH THEY HAVE*
*A "SET" ATTITUDE - AND A SPECIFIC REASON*
*FOR WHICH THEY ARE EXPLORING IT.*

* *MATERIAL WHOSE MEANING*
*HAS BEEN CLEARLY DEFINED*

*These ideas are based on readings from:*
THE ACT OF CREATION — Koestler
EMOTIONS AND MEMORY — Rappaport

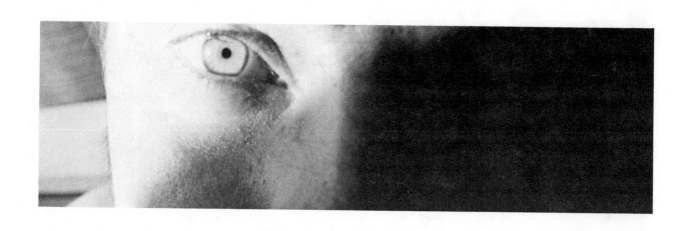

# Scanning

*The eye is like the lens of a camera.*

Focus your mind on the material in front of you, by handling it and thinking about it. Your interest in the outside world is dwindling as you perform this act. You have captured your attention.

Try just holding a stone in your hand. Meditate on its feel, its size, the temperature it projects and its color. You should find that this simple process puts your mind in focus like a camera, aimed at the subject you are thinking about.

Once you learn to put the mind in focus, your memory can become like a photographic plate, absorbing and retaining an impression of the information you are about to read. Try it!

Carefully read the following pages of explanation and example.

*Directed attention does not hypnotize or stupefy in the same way as does enslaved or dispersed attention. But only when learning to withdraw from the task at hand, to maintain a certain thread of awareness which remains apart from thinking, feeling, sensing does one get a taste of fourth stage consciousness. The attention, though directed to whatever the task at hand is at the same time flexible and open, not rigid and narrow.*
— THE MASTER GAME
By Robert S. De Ropp

# Instructions.

Choose an easy book or news article, then follow my instructions.

**Scan entire article at 10 seconds per column.**

**Phase I.**

[1.] Use "The Quest" hand motion.

[2.] Close eyes and think about all the words you've just seen.

[3.] Place the correct words in the "Star Mandala". [See next page.]

**Now go back to the beginning . . . underline the *first line* of each paragraph.**

**Phase II.**

[1.] Close your eyes again and think how the information just read can be added to the "Star".

[a.] Are things starting to make some sense?

[b.] Have you found out some of the names of characters, or where the story takes place, or what is going on?

[2.] Fill in more fully your Star Pattern.

**THE GOAL** is simply to see how much information you've retained using Phase I and II as you scan your article.

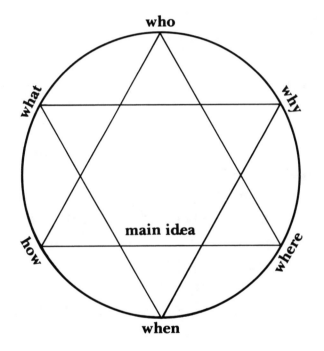

"The Star"

[a] Fill in after scanning.
[b] Add to after reading first line of each paragraph.
[c] Keep simply to one or two word answers.
[d] Add extra lines if you want to add more information.
[e] Sometimes, there will be blank spaces. Some reading materials only have *who* or *what* or *where* but not *how* or *why*.

## Scanning:

At this point, you might say to yourself, "I'm going so fast, these words are just passing my brain without registering any meaning." Here is a way to overcome that misconception. Close your book. Now think about the section you have just scanned. Say some of the words you have seen, silently or aloud. Speak to a friend or relative who is helping you to learn speed reading. If you just try you will be very surprised to find out that you have registered many more words than you were conscious of before you stopped to think about it. Now, open your book again and quickly check, paragraph by paragraph, until you reach the end. Did you really miss anything? Or is it just that you are unsure of yourself and your own real perception.

Relax and let the material sink in and soon it will reappear in your conscious mind. Trust yourself and have patience.

As surely as you believe, so then, it is true for you.

**Practice scanning on all that you intend to read.**

It is difficult to think and remember, if one is out of touch with one's own 'Mind Machine.' *Knowing* what your mind is capable of *creates an ability* from within to perform *any* feat you may previously have thought to be impossible. That mysterious person with the photographic mind, or that genius we all seem to envy, is within us all. Use your newfound abilities, *believe in them. Trust them* and *they are yours!*

— Motherly advice

**Do something active with the material you are about to read.**

Why is this rule so important? First of all, if you read with no purpose and do not use the material in some way, you will most likely forget fifty percent of what you have just read within half an hour, and eighty percent within twenty-four hours. In some cases, these figures are really an underestimate. Can you really count how many times you have had to re-read material you have just read within minutes?

What exactly does, "Do something active with the material," mean? As we have said before, this means one of three things. Repeat important ideas or words to yourself, mentally or verbally. Or, decide that you want to tell someone — your wife, husband, friend, teacher, club members — about the material you are reading when next you see them. Both of these methods allow a certain awareness to take place — a signal to the brain of sorts — which enables you to both concentrate and retain what you are reading to a greater degree than if you used no method at all. You will remember what you have read for a much longer time if you use these methods of recall, either the mental or verbal. But the most effective method by far is **written recall notes**. These are our **memory mandalas**. Turn to the next section to see what mandalas can do for your memory.

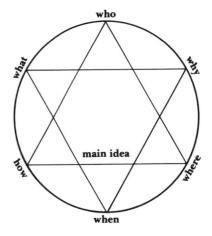

1. Select Book
2. Section off portion you are to read.
3. Hold Book properly.
4. Scan titles back and front flaps, whole chapter or article. Look for answers.
5. Go to beginning and read using Underlining.
6. Practice.

Phacelia crenulata

GREAT RED PAINTBRUSH

# *Step III*

## *Mandalas   —   Practice Stories and Examples*

# MANDALAS

## Memory mandalas.

### *A new system of note-taking — shorter, easier to read, interesting to see, and a suggestive trigger for your memory storehouse.*

*Stimulation of right and left hemispheres of the brain are evident when, you, the reader, logically write in information on each mandala after scanning and reading, while mentally placing that information within the creative portion of the mandala. Using more of your brain power can raise your IQ with regular and increasing exercise of both hemispheres of the brain. Mandalas will help.*

The "Memory Mandala" patterns, dear student, are designed to acquaint you with taking notes in a new way. Your own creative powers will make each mandala more personal, so please feel free to design and construct any pattern that makes you feel more "in touch" with material you read.

I have a few suggestions and breakdowns on the following pages.

## Enhance your memory by adding a simple memory symbol.

What in the world is a memory symbol? Simple. It is a good way of writing down what you have just read while it is still fresh in your mind. In the past, you either did not take notes because it was too much bother, or else you did takes notes and they looked like this:

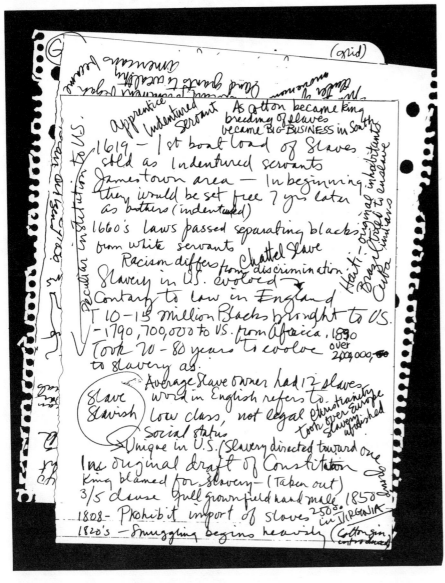

Never again will you have to write notes in this old, messy, long and boring way! Now, let's go on to one powerful system of taking notes.

*Sir Herbert Read, philosopher of art, tells us we are living through a revolution so fundamental that we must search through many past centuries for a parallel. Possibly the only comparable change was the one that took place between the Old and the New Stone Age.*
— FUTURE SHOCK
By Alvin Toffler

# MANDALAS

MANDALA is a Sanscrit word meaning circle. It is defined as a graphic mystic symbol of the universe that is typically in the form of a circle enclosing a square and often containing symetrically arranged representations of deities.

Carl Jung, a pioneer in the field of subconscious intelligence, writes, "Only gradually did I discover what the Mandala really is: formation, transformation, eternal mind's eternal recreation. . . . . my Mandalas were cryptograms in which I saw the self, that is, my whole being actively at work. I had the distinct feeling that they were something central, and in time I acquired through them a living conception of the self.

I saw that everything, all the paths I had been following, all the steps I had been taking, were leading back to a single point—namely to a midpoint. It became plain to me that the Mandala is the center. It is the exponent of all paths. It is the path to the center."

In one of his last works, when he was in his eighties, called "Flying Saucers, a Modern Myth", Jung showed that the Mandala is the preeminent figure for our time. He wrote that the psychological experience that is associated with the UFO is a vision of a round symbol of wholeness. Mandalas usually appear in situations of psychic confusion and perplexity, he wrote, as an: "archetype" which represents a pattern of order. The Mandala, like a psychological "viewfinder, marked with a cross or circle divided into four is superimposed onto the psychic chaos so that each content falls into place and the weltering confusion is held together by the protective circle."

A mandala is meant to aid concentration by narrowing down the psychic field of vision and restricting it to the center. Usually, the mandala contains three circles painted in black or dark blue. They are usually meant to shut out the outside world and hold the inside together. The center is the essential object or goal of contemplation. "The goal of contemplating the processes depicted in the mandala is ... to become inwardly aware of the Deity."

Jung practiced psychological therapy using mandalas. Many of the patients drew mandalas which, surprisingly, repeated several common forms even though they came from a wide variety of people.

"Without going into therapeutic details," he wrote, "I would like to say that a rearranging of the personality is involved, a kind of new centering. That is why mandalas most often appear in connection with chaotic psychic states of disorientation or panic. They then have the purpose of reducing the confusion to order, though this is never the conscious intention of the patient. At all events, they express order, balance and wholeness. Patients themselves often emphasize the beneficial or soothing effects of such pictures. Most mandalas have an intuitive irrational character and through their symbolic content exert a retroactive influence on the unconscious. They therefore possess a magical significance like icons, whose possible efficacy is never consciously felt by the patient. There are repetitions of motifs in many patients, marked similarities in drawings done by the most diverse patients." Jung said that these ideas, which were unknown to their creators were "archetypes." He said they were part of a collective unconscious.

*Reasoning, reverie, dreaming, imagination, planning, insight – what do these thought activities have in common? They are alike in that they all enable the individual to deal with objects and events of the outside world which are no longer present – to deal with the environment in the form of symbols.*
*— THINKING*
By Karl U. Smith

# Using a mandala —
## *the simplest step.*

**Let's again try the Star Mandala.**

Our first mandala form is meant to show you how to find the very basics in a reading selection — the who, what, when, where, why and how, as well as the main idea.

[1] Draw a six pointed star:

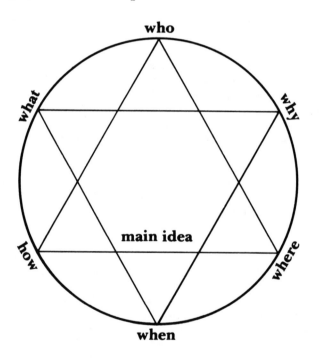

[2] Now, add at the tip of each point of the star the simple words **who, what, when, where, why** and **how.** Leave the midsection blank, as this is where you will write the main idea in a few simple words.

Now, draw a large circle around the star.

*The outstanding memory which some geniuses are said to have possessed may be possibly due to their many-dimensioned ways of analyzing and storing experiences.*
— THE ACT OF CREATION
By Arthur Koestler

[3] Now **scan** the *whole* selection on the following page, using either your circular or quest hand motion. Don't spend more than ten seconds. Remember, you are to scout the territory for its *general* tone and content, and what *you* think *you* can get from it. Now close your eyes and ask yourself — what do I already know about this subject or author? What do I most want to get from the material? How should I approach the reading? Is it serious or light, do the details matter or the general content? Get some idea of why the material was written, and how it's organized. Can you grasp the theme or subject, can you establish a point of view towards reading it? Before you open your eyes, **think about** *who, what, when, where, why, how* **and** *main idea* **as they are written on your star.**

**Open your eyes, but do not look at the selection just yet. Now, if any of these points were clear to you after your first scan, then quickly jot them down on your star pattern.**

**[See next page.]**

**Our reading selection is taken from the book** *Touch the Earth,* **by T. C. McCluhan. It is quoted from the autobiography of Black Elk, a holy man of the Ogalala tribe of Dakota Sioux. In his youth, Black Elk had been instructed by the great priests of his tribe in the sacred traditions of his people:**

You have noticed that everything the Indian does is in a circle and that is because the power of the world always works in circles and everything tries to be round. In the old days, when we were a strong and happy people, all of our power came to us from the sacred hoop of the nation, and so long as the hoop was unbroken, the people flourished. The flowering tree was the living center of the hoop, and the circle of the four quarters nourished it. The East gave peace and light, the South gave warmth, the West gave rain and the North with its mighty wind and cold gave strength and endurance. This knowledge came to us from the outer world with our religion. Everything the power of the world does is in a circle. The sky is round, and I have heard that the earth is round like a ball and so are all the stars. The wind in its greatest power, whirls. Birds make their nests in circles, for theirs is the same religion as ours. The sun comes forth and goes down again in a circle. The moon does the same and both are round. Even the seasons form a great circle in their changing and always come back again to where they were. The life of a man is a circle, from childhood to childhood, and so it is in everything where power moves. Our tipis were round like the nests of birds and these were always set in a circle, the nation's hoop, a nest of many nests where the great spirit meant for us to hatch our children.

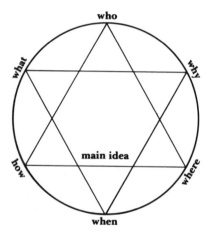

Notice this selection has only one paragraph. Most articles and stories have more than one.

I chose this selection for its beauty.

[4] Now, go back and underline just the **first few lines of every paragraph.** Why? The first line is usually the key to every paragraph. When you have finished scanning the first lines, close your eyes again and try to remember what was said. Are there any main ideas, words, characters or events that stayed with you? Can you fill in any more points of the star? If so, do so quickly, without looking back at the selection. Learn to trust your perception and memory.

[5] It is now time to read the text fully using your underlining technique.

**Remember:**

Let your hand be the conductor for your eyes and mind, setting a pace equal to your understanding of **phrases**, not individual words. Concentrate on using your peripheral vision while you read. Be conscious that you are reading with purpose — in order to find the answers to the questions written on the star. This time concentrate for **meaning** — what is the main idea the author is trying to get across to you? When you have finished reading, close your eyes and think carefully about what you have gained from reading. Then write down the answers around and inside of the star mandala. Be neat. Stay within the circle.

[6] Now, go back and scan again. This is *re*-**scanning. Ten seconds only — but this time look for only what you have missed in the earlier steps, those details you could not find.**

[Study carefully.]

# Review.

**Methods of remembering reading material:**
*Mental:* You think about it.
*Oral:* You say it. This reinforces the thought impression.
*Written:* The most reliable insurance of remembering. This has been proven by experiments on memory and perception.

**The importance of purpose.**

You, the reader, are the final judge of how you want to read the material, and this is a direct reflection of *why* you are reading it. **Keep your purpose in mind.** It focuses your thought. It clarifies your comprehension. It screens your impressions so that only the most useable and relevant information *for your purpose* penetrates your mind. Whether you are reading for leisure time enjoyment, to pass an examination, to fill an information gap, through curiosity or necessity, will be reflected by the rate at which you read, what you wish to remember, and your method of taking notes. Your intention will set your reading style. Scan with clear intention. Read according to your ascertained needs. This is reading with purpose. Reading, with a clear direction, increases absorption and helps you to stow away information and knowledge.

# Use easy materials.

It has been proven by those of us who developed these techniques, that the use of **easy reading materials** in the beginning stages allows students to develop confidence in their new reading habits and to build speed and comprehension over a period of time. Later, you will see how easy it will be to read faster on more technical or complex materials. Right now, however, you must think almost as though you are muscle-building in your mind. Body-builders begin with smaller weights, and as their muscles grow, the size of the weights is increased. The mind is not a muscle, but it has the ability to improve with exercise. Speed readers learn to balance hand motion with eye contact and thereby build comprehension. A complex book is too heavy a weight to begin with. Start light, and build up your mind until it is ready to handle heavy material. *You'll soon enough be reading even the most technical books.*

The stories that follow are merely *examples* to read and to use in practicing your newly found skills. Business and professional people can use materials related to their specific professions (please see technical reports and journals following this section).

*Each story and example is followed by a practice story and mandalas for you to try.*

# Can a whale find life
# in the desert?

The sperm whale is a curious creature. Its head, as big and cavernous as a freight car, is filled with a mixture of solid, white wax called spermaceti and a liquid wax called sperm oil. Why an animal should have a head full of wax and oil is unknown, but it and the blubber, which is the greatest source of oil, are the cause of sperm whale hunting.

The wax and oil have properties that are important to industry, and a large sperm whale may yield several tons of each. The sperm whale is the only current source of such chemicals; industry has tried and failed to synthesize them economically, and no other plentiful animal produces an oil with anything like the chemical structure of sperm oil. No plant produces one either. No plant other than jojoba, that is.

In 1935, research chemists at the University of Arizona found that the oil of the jojoba was made from molecules entirely unlike those of oils made by any other plant. Soybeans, corn, peanuts, olive trees, and all the rest build their oils by combining glycerol with fatty acids. But isolated in the Sonoran Desert, jojoba followed its own evolution. Its cells and enzymes produce absolutely no glycerol. Instead, they combine fatty alcohols with fatty acids to form a vegetable oil having unique molecular shape and size, and with unusual properties.

Why a plant left the mainstream of evolution to produce a different fat — one of the basic building blocks of life — is not known. That it is virtually identical with sperm oil is one of nature's greatest coincidences. For sperm whale survival, it may be crucial.

Millions of jojoba bushes dot the slopes and flats of perhaps 100,000 square miles of Arizona, southern California and Mexico. Each shrub struggles for existence in a barren, inhospitable world where some years rain may not fall at all. Jojoba is a woody, upright shrub with the size and stature of a suburban hedge plant. In parched desert areas it struggles to reach a spindly two feet, but in better-watered locations it may grow to be six or eight feet tall. Green and verdant in good locations, the leaves glaze to a metallic blue-green under the stress of drought. But only one foot of annual rainfall is needed for the commercial production of jojoba seed; even four inches will produce a crop.

Jojoba plants are either male or female. Males have clusters of capsules that, in a timed-release fashion, fling pollen into the wind during a six-week period in the spring. Once pollinated, the inconspicuous leaf-like flowers on the female bushes begin forming green, olivelike fruit that, in the heat of summer, mature, dry out, and drop their peanut-sized seeds onto the ground.

The soft, wrinkled, dark-brown seeds ooze oil if they are squeezed. They are half oil. The standard techniques for extracting peanut oil, soybean oil, olive oil and others can be used to separate the light-yellow jojoba oil; then simple refining purifies it to a clear, colorless oil with almost no smell.

Oil from the sperm whale is used in the quenching and cold-rolling of steel, in leather dressing, in lubricating high-speed machinery and precision instruments, and in the textile industry. Lubrication is its major use. As the pressures develop between metal parts in gears and heavy machinery, sperm oil, unlike other oils, is unaffected. Treating it with sulfur produces a super-lubricant that, even at extreme pressures, won't squeeze out from between the metal to leave a dry spot that increases friction and wear. How does jojoba oil compare?

The U.S. Army has spent more than a year testing this point. The project director recently showed me their results. On graph after graph, the sperm oil line and the jojoba oil line were virtually imposed. Because of its virtual identity with sperm oil, many researchers now believe jojoba oil will find markets in all the industries that previously used sperm oil.

The Indian tribes associated with the jojoba project have been enthusiastic and encouraging. Jojoba has been used by them for centuries as a cooking oil and hair treatment. Lambert Noline has set up the Apache Marketing Cooperative Association, fashioned after the farmer's cooperatives so successful elsewhere in the country. California Indians have also formed a cooperative — one that will plant and harvest jojoba on several small reservations east of Los Angeles and San Diego. The word about jojoba is leaking out, and already the Indian cooperatives have more orders than they can fill. Keen interest has been shown by several of the nation's largest corporations. And the cooperatives have orders from three large corporations in Japan — which may have important implications for sperm whale survival: Japan's whalers kill the most sperm whales.

Nevertheless, exploiting wild jojoba stands on the reservations is unlikely to meet the demand for the oil. Handpicking the small seeds from the twiggy, rank-growing wild bushes is terrible drudgery. All the harvested seed have to be manhandled out, and snakes shelter in the debris beneath the bushes. Instead, the future of jojoba is as an orchardlike crop, grown where the terrain facilitates harvest, pruning, fertilizing, and pest control. And it will be a long time before jojoba is a crop with pedigreed varieties and predictable behavior. It is still wild. Its genetics are terribly mixed, and to improve it the way we have improved corn and wheat will not be easy. But agronomists are beginning to try. Promising leads are appearing and there is nothing to suggest that jojoba can't be domesticated.

In international commerce, jojoba oil, with its chemical identity to sperm oil, can probably enter the same commercial channels as sperm oil. If it can underprice sperm oil, as seems likely with the rising expense of sending ships, planes, helicopters, and large crews to hunt the ever-decreasing whales, it should be able to capture the whole market. Luckily, sperm whale meat is virtually inedible and contributes little to the profits of whaling. Thus, if the market for sperm oil is removed, the incentive for sperm whaling will disappear. Then this desert plant will give life to the sperm whales. The animals will live and multiply in peace.

— Excerpted from *The Audubon Cause* in *Audubon* magazine, September, 1975.
  By Noel D. Vietmeyer

*Now that you have begun to use all the tools of reading (Decisions, Scanning and Underlining), you are ready for the final touches.*

*'The Tree" Mandala or Large Mandala is used 'only' after scanning and filling in the Star. The following stories with example Mandalas filled in, should be carefully examined. Follow* **all** *steps in their* **exact order.** *Do yourself a big favor and* **do not skip any steps,** *and your rewards will encompass great comprehension and superb memory retention. (You will truly amaze yourself).*

**— Motherly Advice**

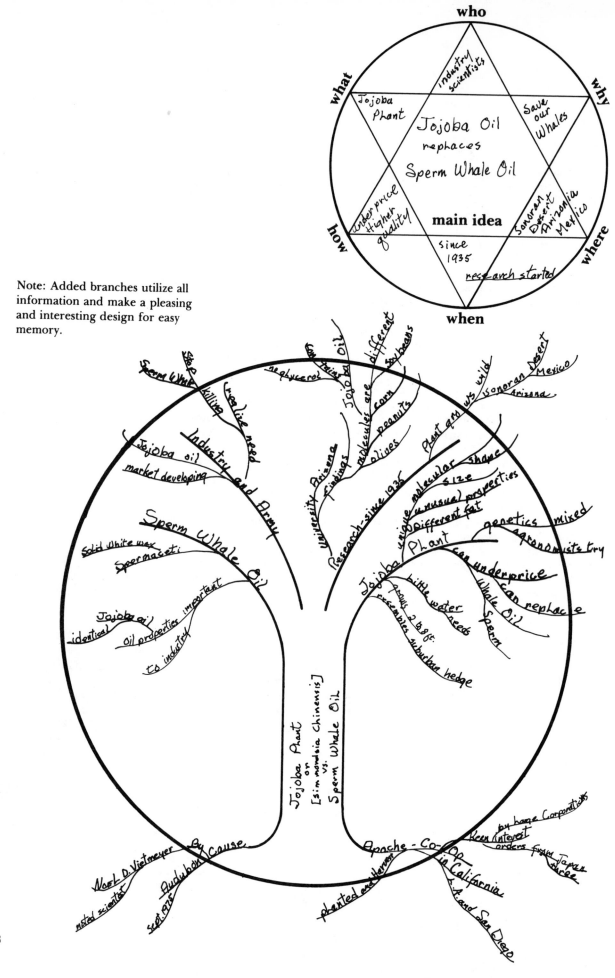

Note: Added branches utilize all information and make a pleasing and interesting design for easy memory.

**Sample stories
on the next pages
are for your practice.**

# Say "Rooo-beee!"

I went down to Ruby's pen. She was waiting, watching me out of one soft, slightly sad brown eye. I waded in up to my ankles and she swam to me. I rubbed her head and snout for a few minutes.

I got the ball and tossed it into Ruby's pen. She immediately understood that this was catch, and after nosing the ball for a few seconds threw it back to me. We tossed it back and forth until Ruby convinced me that she was in the mood for a game.

It occurred to me that I could use this game of catch as a reward in an attempt to get Ruby to vocalize. It seemed like an ideal reward; we were both enjoying the game, and her participation was voluntary. I decided to try to get her to mimic her own name. "Ruby," I said. "Say, Rooo-beee!" All I got back at first was a bunch of delphinese, somewhere between a whistle and a squawk. I threw the ball, and she returned it. "All right, now, say 'Ruby'! Rooo-beee!" Again that squawk. "No, you're going to have to do better than that. C'mon, say 'Rooo-beee'!" For several more repetitions all I could get was that squawky noise. I noticed that *she was repeating the same sound every time*; it wasn't just any old squawk, but one with recognizable characteristics. But it was delphinese, which might as well be gibberish to me. I wanted English out of her, or at least a reasonable facsimile, and I was going to withhold the reward until I got it.

Suddenly her vocalization changed. Her squawk came out in two distinct syllables, rather like the way I had been syllabificating "Rooo-beee!" I hurled the ball, and she returned it. Our progress became unbelievably rapid. In the space of five minutes, she began to copy the syllabification, rhythm, tone, and inflections of my pronunciation of the word "Ruby," and she did so with an accuracy and a speed I found amazing. Every time she came closer to my pronunciation I threw the ball, and she would return it to me. Each time her pronunciation was further away from mine I would withhold the ball until she improved. We became completely wrapped up in each other; the outside world ceased to exist. We stood a few feet apart in the water of her pen, staring at each other intently with bright eyes, and the excitement between us was palpable. Never in my life had I known such an intimate feeling of being in contact with an incredible non-human creature. It felt like it was what I had been created to do. Our minds seemed to be running on the same wave. We were together.

Sometimes she would break back down into delphinese, and then I would withhold the ball until she had improved. She put a consonant R sound on the beginning of her squawk; and then she put a Y sound at the end. The result was a startling, eerie mimicry that sounded like my "Rooo-beee!" yet wasn't. The R sound, the Y sound, the tone, the rhythm, syllabification, were all there, but the middle of the sound was still this weird squawk. This all took place in about ten minutes. I was overwhelmed with the speed and accuracy of her learning; I hadn't expected anything like this in response to a simple game of catch.

She repeated the word with this degree of accuracy a couple of times, then started babbling at me in delphinese, shaking her head up and down with her jaws open in that gesture, usually associated with pleasure, that I called "ya-ya-ing." I tried to get her to say "Rooo-beee!" again; more ya-ya-ing. Then she swam back a few feet and made a peculiar noise, a kind of "keee-orr-oop," but about three times faster than you pronounce it. It occurred to me — I don't know why—*to repeat that sound*. Ruby seemed to be expecting it of me. I did the best I could with it. She repeated it, but now it sounded slightly different; I mimicked her changes. God, she's doing to me what I was just doing to her! Where will this lead? By now the ball was forgotten; I was totally absorbed in listening to Ruby's vocalizations and attempting to mimic them as accurately as possible with my inadequate human lips and vocal cords. She repeated the sound again, changed still more, and I copied that; she repeated it again and as I tried to mimic her I thought, this sounds vaguely familiar — "kee-orr-oop." The light in my head went on. *The sound I had just successfully imitated was the one she had been giving to me in the beginning*, in response to my first attempts to make her say "Ruby!"

This realization struck me as the sound was coming out my lips. Several fuses in my mind blew simultaneously and I did an incredible double-take, nearly falling over, and staring at Ruby, who was watching me with great concentration. When she saw the double-take, and knew I knew, *she* flipped out, and went ya-ya-ing around the pool, throwing water into the air, very excited, and apparently happy that this two-legged cousin of hers was progressing so rapidly. I just stood there, watching her, trying to figure out exactly what had just happened between myself and this dolphin.

What do I think the meaning of that experience was? I don't really know. I have *some* ideas, however. In response to an English word, Ruby had given me a delphinese word or phrase, which I had ignored. She succeeded in taking control of the situation—*although I had not been willing to relinquish control*—and had then tricked me into pronouncing the sound I had at first ignored! Our mutual reactions were so spontaneous, and so vivid, that there is no doubt of this in my mind. *I had been the one slowing down the communications between us!* I can't tell you with what force that realization struck me. But what was the meaning of that sound? I can only guess. Certainly Ruby was sophisticated enough to recognize her human name. It occurred to me that she was most likely either telling me her name for *me* — a straight turnabout — or telling me her name for herself. But these are just my projections.

Months later, I was to try and get Ruby to repeat her vocalizations for some friends of mine, with little success. She did manage to enunciate "Rooo-beee!" on or two times, with a precision approaching that of the first time, but it was not the same: she was restless and impatient, and I could not work with her very long. In retrospect, the error lay not with her, but with *me*. Anyone working with dolphins would do well to remember that they have a very low threshold of boredom, and once they have mastered something, they want to go on to something new. You, as a "human being" however, will probably be so surprised that you will want the dolphin to repeat its behavior over and over again until your mind, dulled by years of exposure to social and educational systems, finally starts to believe what is being told: this sleek gray creature in the water wants to *communicate* with you.

— Excerpted from "Say 'Rooo-beee!'" by Malcolm Brenner, in his book *In Contact: An Interspecies Romance* from *Mind in the Waters* by Joan McIntyre

**Remember to use underlining on *all* reading materials.**

*A large, complex brain implies large, complex capabilities and a mental sensitivity. Such capabilities and sensitivities can exist of course in forms we have not yet recognized." John Lilly, M.D., Ph.D., trained in neurology, neurophysiology and psychoanalysis, discussing dolphin brains in relationship to the human mind.*

— MIND IN THE WATERS
Assembled by Joan McIntyre

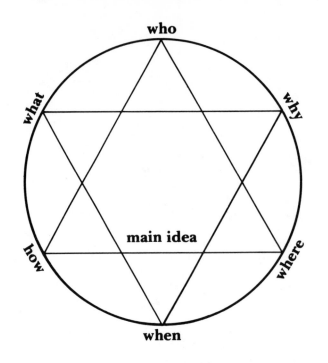

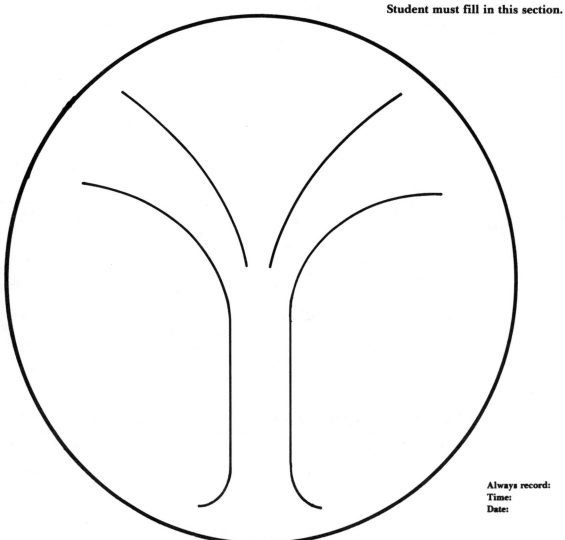

Student must fill in this section.

Always record:
Time:
Date:

**Notice the different patterns
within the circle mandala.
Each is an authentic and ancient
Indian sign meaning health,
happiness and good fortune.**

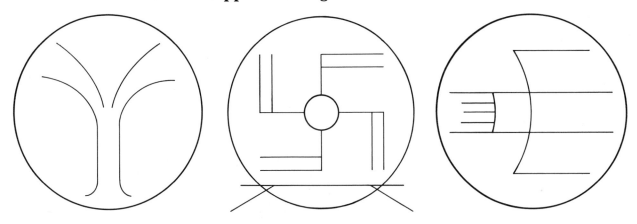

Stimulation of right and left hemispheres of the brain are evident when, you, the reader, logically write in information on each mandala after scanning and reading, while mentally placing that information within the creative portion of the mandala. Using more of your brain power can raise your IQ with regular and increasing exercise of both hemispheres of the brain. Mandalas will help.

There are many reasons why I chose the stories in this section on developing your memory. All stem from my deep love of all living things and my concern for our continued existence. I felt, too, that all living beings have special interest in each other, whether conscious or unconscious, and that the survival of humanity on this planet depends upon all creatures being given the space they need in order to maintain dignity, intelligence and wholeness.

**More sample stories
on the next pages
for your practice.**

# The touching.

To Touch and Feel is to Experience. Many people live out their entire lives without ever really Touching or being Touched by anything. These people live within a world of mind and imagination that may move them sometimes to joy, tears, happiness or sorrow. But these people never really Touch. They do not live and become one with life.

The Sun Dancer believes that each person is a unique Living Medicine Wheel, powerful beyond imagination, that has been limited and placed on this earth to Touch, Experience and Learn. The Six Grandfathers taught me that each man, woman, and child at one time was a Living Power that existed somewhere in time and space. These Powers were without form, but they were aware. They were alive.

Each Power possessed boundless energy and beauty. These living Medicine Wheels were capable of nearly anything. They were beautiful and perfect in all ways except one. They had no understanding of limitation, no experience of substance. These Beings were total energy of the Mind, without Body or Heart. They were placed upon this earth that they might Learn the things of the Heart through Touching.

According to the Teachers, there is only one thing that all people possess equally. This is their loneliness. No two people on the face of this earth are alike in any one thing except for their loneliness. This is the cause of our Growing, but it is also the cause of our wars. Love, hate, greed and generosity are all rooted within our loneliness, within our desire to be needed and loved.

The only way that we can overcome our loneliness is through Touching. It is only in this way that we can learn to be Total Beings. God is a presence of this Total. *Heamavihio*, the Breath of Wisdom, and *Miaheyyun*, Total Understanding, are but two of the words in the Cheyenne language which express this Wholeness.

— Excerpted from *Seven Arrows* By Hyemeyohsts Storm

*The Medicine Wheel Circle is the Universe. It is change, life, death, birth and learning. This Great Circle is the lodge of our bodies, our minds, and our hearts. It is the cycle of all things that exist. The Circle is our Way of Touching, and of experiencing Harmony with every other thing around us. And for those who seek Understanding the Circle is their Mirror. This Circle is the Flowering Tree.*

— SEVEN ARROWS
By Hyemeyohsts Storm

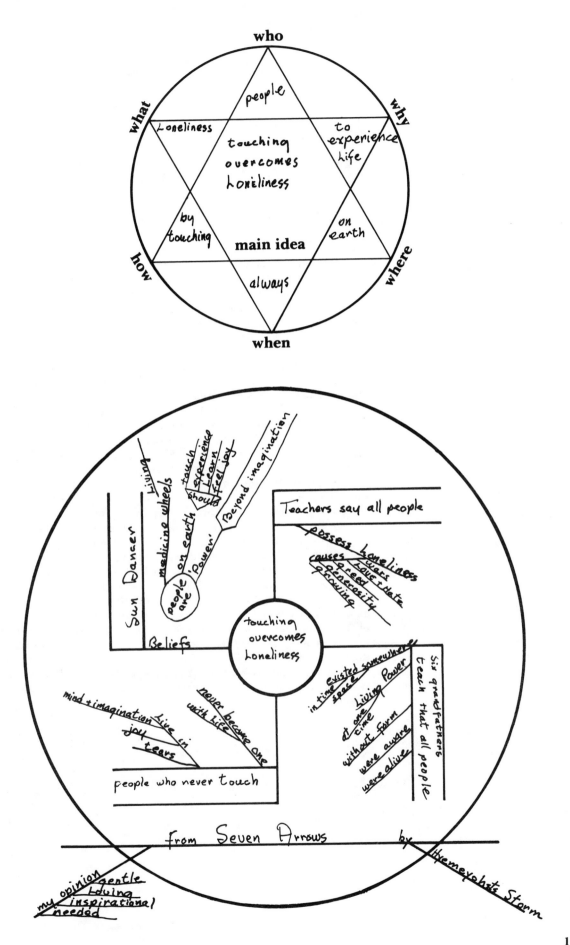

**who**

people

**what**
Loneliness

**why**
to experience life

touching
overcomes
Loneliness

by touching

on earth

**main idea**

**how**

always

**where**

**when**

Sun Dancer

Living

medicine wheels

touch
experience
learn
feel joy
should
'Power'
on earth
people are

Beyond imagination

Beliefs

Teachers say all people

possess Loneliness
causes wars
have + hate
greed
generosity
growing

touching
overcomes
Loneliness

existed somewhere
in time space
Living Power
at one time
without form
were aware
were alive

Six grandfathers
teach that all people

mind + imagination
Live in
joy
tears

never became one
with life

people who never touch

from Seven Arrows

by

Hyemeyohsts Storm

my opinion
gentle
Living
inspirational
needed

# The man who didn't follow trails, but made them.

Of all the rough-and-ready mountain men gathered on the Green River for the fur trappers' rendezvous of 1833, the toughest and most picturesque was Joseph Reddeford Walker. Then 34 years old, Walker was in his physical prime and cut a truly impressive figure. He measured six feet tall, weighed more than 200 pounds and was blue-eyed and handsome in a craggy, hawk-beaked way. He wore his hair long in the Indian style, had a full beard, and, in the fashion of his time and place, he was something of a clotheshorse. Even among so many colorful figures, and in the midst of a wild rendezvous, Joe Walker stood out as a kind of beau ideal of the mountain man.

This year Joe Walker had something very interesting to say to the fur men assembled at Green River: he called for men to join him on an expedition into the dimly known, trackless lands to the west, perhaps all the way from the rendezvous site to the coast of California. Walker's announcement created a sensation. Such a trip had been tried only thrice before — by another mountain man, Jedediah Smith, in 1826 and 1827, and in 1829 by Peter Ogden, an energetic leader in the Hudson's Bay Company. Smith and Ogden had followed more or less the same southern route into California — a route which was neither direct nor safe, taking them across bleak desert lands.

Joe Walker's prestige as a frontiersman would grow steadily throughout his life. For fifty years, spanning the whole period from the rise of the mountain men to the coming of the cowboys, he roamed the trans-Mississippi country from the Rockies to Mexico, from desert to ocean, leading his own expeditions. He was a geographical genius with a remarkable intuitive sense for the shape, texture and topographical details of the Western wilderness.

The expedition to California would test to the utmost Walker's gift for making trails. The Great Basin had been seen and noted as a terrible looking place, but its extent and the nature of its western boundary were matters of surmise. There was particular confusion about the relationship between the Rockies and the Sierra Nevada. The Sierra had often been seen from the California side, but its size and difficulty were greatly underestimated. Joe Walker and his party would soon learn the truth about this formidable chain of mountains.

Walker's trek to California, one of the most fruitful explorations ever conducted by a mountain man, was typical of his endeavors — a model of good planning and efficiency. Walker and his men left the trappers' rendezvous on the Green River ... each man mounted and each leading three additional horses packed with every article necessary for the comfort of men engaged in an expedition of this kind.

Actually the abundance of horses was a kind of trademark for any party led by Joe Walker. Of all the mountain men, Walker seems to have been the best and most knowledgeable stockman. Unlike most mountain men, he had horse sense in the literal meaning of the words: he used animals often, used them carefully, took pains to find enough forage for them and did not ride them into the ground — though like all Western explorers he regarded spare animals as emergency rations, and knew that on the hard trails and high mountains he would inevitably lose some of his stock.

On the Bear River, four days after they had left the rendezvous, Walker halted the group while they were still in well-watered, wooded country and set them to hunting. He kept them at this work until each man had added 60 pounds of dried and jerked meat to his pack. Ordinary mountain men probably would have neglected this elementary precaution. They tended to gorge themselves on a day when hunting was easy, then starve a week later when they could not find game.

Walker's prudence was again displayed when he reached the Salt Lake vicinity. Here he adopted a tactic used by all his successful predecessors, from Coronado to Lewis and Clarke. He stopped, sought out a band of local Indians and interrogated them on the character of the country and the best routes west. Combining the advice he received from these Bannock Indians with the earlier rumors he had heard about the Great Basin, he sifted all of the information through his intuitive sense of what simply smelled right, and finally picked a route that proved to be the best possible one through the desolate country.

    — Excerpted from *The Trailblazers*, by Bill Gilbert,
        Time-Life Books, 1973.

**Remember to use underlining on *all* reading materials.**

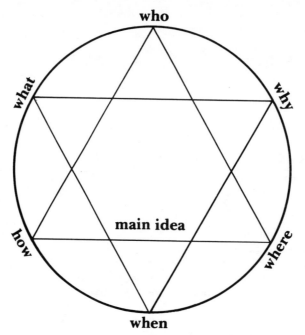

**Student must fill in this section.**

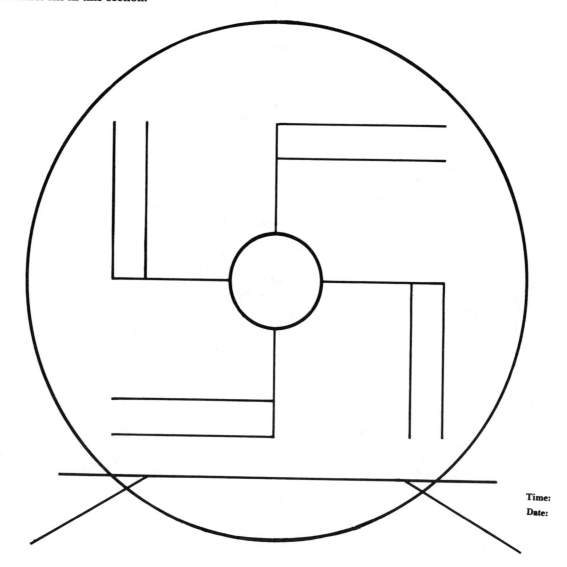

Time:

Date:

# Like tin cats in a shooting gallery.

Once upon a long time ago the mountain lion was one of the most spectacular members of the wildlife community in North America. Those days are gone.

The mountain lion — puma, cougar, or panther — has the greatest north-south range of any cat in the world. They are still found from almost the southern tip of South America up into Canada. Over most of their original range in North America they have been totally extirpated. And in South America, where there are still good populations of these beautiful cats, their days are numbered.

The mountain lion can survive under an incredible range of habitat circumstances. But it has not been the lot of the mountain lion to be left alone. The hand of man has been raised against it at every turn. ... To be sure, there have been renegades who deserved their fate. Any naturally predatory animal, including man, produces an inevitable number of criminals that must be destroyed or removed to where they can do no harm. But we have continued to harass, harm and destroy *all* of our predators because of the damage done by a few. The mountain lion, the wolf, the bear, the coyote, the lynx, the bobcat, the hawks and the eagles all have felt the full blast of human wrath and ignorance. They will all soon be extinct. The coyote, the black bear and the bobcat will outlast the rest by perhaps as much as thirty years. The others do not stand a chance.

The men's magazines still run pieces every year with lurid art showing enormous pumas leaping from trees clawing men and horses to the ground already littered with the carcasses of hunting dogs mauled and mutilated by the blood crazed-cat. It is pure nonsense. In all of North American history there are something like 13 or 14 records of unprovoked attacks by mountain lions. In most cases, the animals were rabid. In a few others, the animals weighed under 50 pounds and were obviously cubs who had lost their mothers before they learned to hunt and were wild with despair and hunger. The mountain lion in the wild, unmolested, is a perfectly harmless cat as far as human life is concerned.

It is hardly necessary to wax poetic about the beauty of these creatures, or about the place they have in the wildlife picture. They are predators and only the most totally uninformed person today does not know that predators are the stone on which nature sharpens the muscle and wit of prey animals. Without a normal quota of predators in an ecosystem, all the animals in that system are in deep trouble.

What we *can* say is that the world needs its mountain lions. This planet will be incredibly poorer for their loss. All of the other animals will become weaker with each generation until the ultimate tragedy of final extinction of everything wild takes place. It must be made against the law to shoot or otherwise molest a mountain lion — without a Federal license to destroy a proven stock killer.

Will this happen? Will the mountain lion receive protection and our permission to repopulate part of its original range? If it does not, if it does not happen *soon*, then the mountain lion will be gone, forever, and with it goes one of the last traces of human morality.

— Excerpted from "Like Tin Cats in a Shooting Gallery," by Roger Caras in *Earth*, November 1971.

**Fill in *only* after scanning and reading titles and first lines of paragraphs.**

**Notice that I leave occasional empty spaces.**

**See the way each added line pertains only to that thought.**

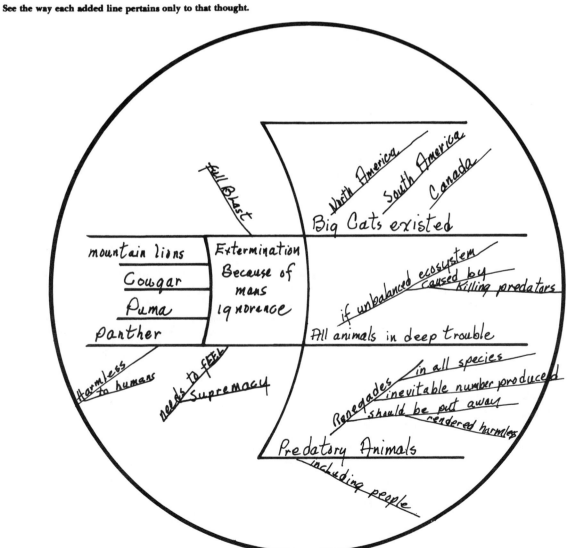

# Wolves versus moose
# on Isle Royale.

**Remember to use underlining on *all* reading materials.**

That rare sound, the timber wolf's haunting *owoo-oo-oo*, came to our ears one iron-cold February night on Isle Royale, in Lake Superior. The lead cantor was an impressive basso. His low pitched moaning set off the others, who joined in on higher notes with drawn-out whoops and wails, yips and yipes — and yes, even barks, although some have said that wolves never bark.

At intervals there were chummy duets, melodious arias, and rambling obbligatos. Then a mass chorale of resounding splendor.

I couldn't help thinking of the adjectives commonly applied to wolf howling: horrible, eerie, blood-chilling, demoniac. Not so. For us, this was the only time we heard a concert, with all stops out, from close at hand. For us, it was a thrilling fulfillment of the wilderness setting — the grand opera of primitive nature.

The performance went on for about ten minutes, then trailed off into afterthought howls and whines. All was silent on the ridge. The only sound was the thump and thud of ice straining against the rocky shore. Then we realized we were shivering.

Around the coffeepot at our long table, we relived our experience and Roy raised a question that may have bothered us all: "The way the world is headed," he remarked, "I wonder how many people will ever get to hear what we heard tonight."

"As far as the United States is concerned," said Dave, "if they don't hear it in Alaska or Minnesota, they won't stand a chance." He referred to the little-known plight of the gray, or timber, wolf. In all the United States south of Alaska, only northern Minnesota harbors a reasonably safe breeding population of wolves. The long-harrassed animals of upper Michigan and Wisconsin are down to perhaps a couple of dozen. Whether they are breeding is uncertain; they seen to be on the way out. Occasional stragglers may cross our boundaries from Canada or Mexico, but these soon go the way of their trapped and poisoned forerunners. The truth is the Lobo is gone from nearly all his old haunts.

For three winters, we tracked wolves for hundreds of miles, along well-traveled ice-shelves, over lakes and bays, and on ridgetop trails. We watched *Canis lupus* in every phase of daily activity: trekking, sleeping, playing, mating, and hunting and killing moose.

During the season of open water, adult moose may be especially difficult to kill; an alerted moose can avoid trouble by wading in so deep the wolves would have to swim to attack. But this relative safety of water vanishes with the coming of deep snows.

Healthy, vigorous moose survive attack in two ways. Some stand and fight. Others, as soon as they see wolves, head off across country at their rapid, long-legged trot. Struggling through deep snow, wolves may keep up for as much as two or three miles, but eventually they lie panting in defeat.

Once while observing wolves, we saw they had approached to within a few yards of a cow and calf. Protecting her calf, the cow defiantly faced the pack. As the wolves approached, she leaped at them, lashing out furiously with her forefeet. We could sense her anger as, with ears laid back and mane erect, she held her ground.

The wolves got the message, too. They scattered in panic before each charge, then stood around considering. After several minutes, to our surprise they abruptly left and went south.

Must not be hungry, I mused.

Not until later did we recognize this to be common behavior. The wolves have a prudent fear of their dangerous quarry. They frequently give up and move on when a moose deliberately stands and defies them. We found that the pack stalks or tests about twelve moose for every one they kill.

—Excerpted from "Wolves Versus Moose on Isle Royale," by D.L. Allen and L.D. Mech, *National Geographic*, February 1963.

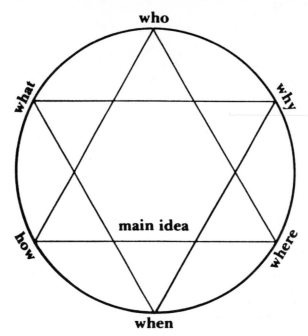

who

what

why

main idea

how

where

when

**Student must fill in this section.**

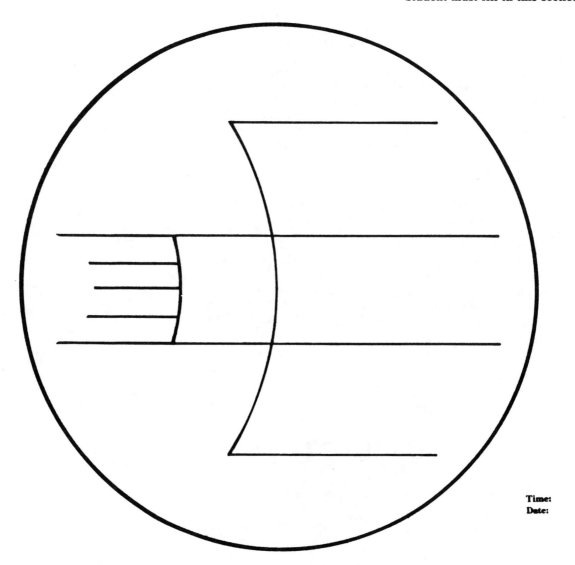

**Time:**
**Date:**

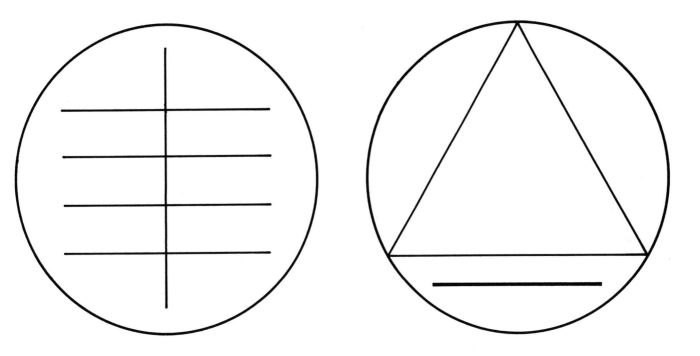

Here are two pages of mandalas, taken from authentic American Indian designs. They will help stimulate your exploration of different shapes and sizes. You, dear student, must read and remember your readings, and then create designs that appeal to your *own* senses and which will help you remember the readings.

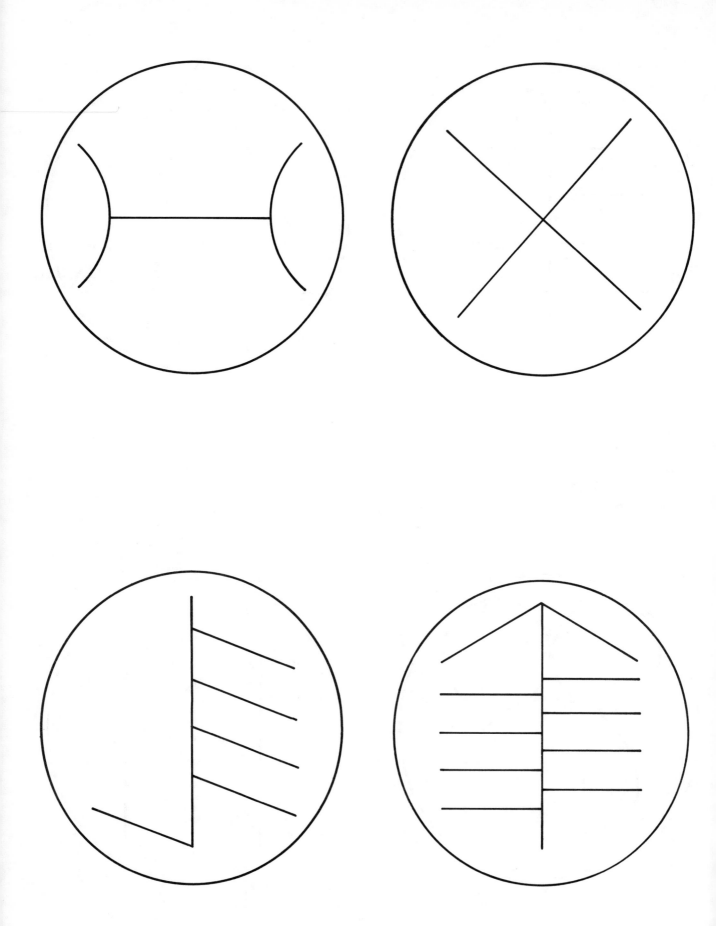

# Using and refining
# what you now know.

The new-born infant lives, in William James' words, in a "blooming, buzzing confusion — a world of sensation without organization." It cannot analyze, code and match new inputs with the appropriate responses. Similarly, when you read without organization, you cannot permanently store the information. You cannot respond to it and you usually have difficulty understanding the meaning quickly. The "star pattern" questions help you to exert a selective control over the "input" — the words you are reading. This gives you a focus to help you interpret the material. The simplicity of the ideas you are searching for aids your recall; the pattern you write them down in creates mental organization, re-organization and synthesis. The circular mandala shape promotes a feeling of centeredness. Your personal mandalas help you to isolate the main ideas from the support material. Select mandala forms that feel appropriate to what you have read. Use your star mandala as a reference for filling out your new mandala. If there are several main ideas in a chapter, then use linking mandalas. You will be manipulating the material until it acquires a simple form which is **easy for you to remember, visually, logically and emotionally**. When you construct a mandala, you are determining the value of the material to you — your personal response to it. Your judgment of what is most significant in the material — what the overall main idea or ideas are, what is the supportive data, what are the connecting links — all will determine how you construct your mandala. But always choose shapes in the circle that most appeal to **you** when making your mandala.

The following pages break down the different types of materials that are available for reading. Each breakdown summarizes the material in terms of its type, usual purpose, format and typical examples. These summaries are to help you become familiar with materials you do not yet read as well as to conveniently analyze the characteristics of many types of reading matter. We hope these summaries will simplify your reading and allow you to vary your approach as we will suggest.

Different materials require different approaches. You will not read philosophy in the same way as an instruction manual — you will have different purposes and therefore different ways of relating to the material. Consequently, your speed should also vary, and the type of mandala you choose should reflect the needs you set for yourself in the reading, as well as the mood of the material.

**Remember to use underlining on *all* reading materials.**

*People Everywhere Read . . .*

*. . . as a diversion*

*. . . direction for future plans*

*. . . to interest others in learning*

. . . for fun

*. . . precious family moments*

. . . *for family togetherness*

. . . for the simple Love of it

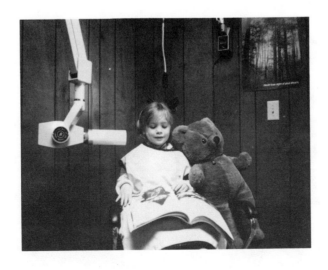

*. . . a natural environment for study*

*. . . find a quiet place for practice*

. . . *to entertain others*

. . . *for new information*

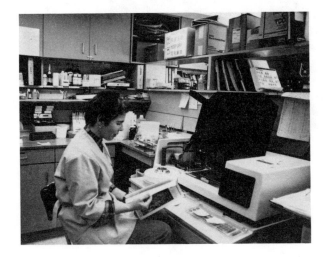

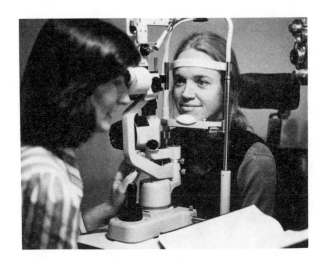

*. . . for tranquil moments*

REDWOOD SORREL

# Step IV

## How to Handle Different Reading Materials

*The rate at which man has been storing up useful knowledge about himself and the universe has been spiralling upward for 10,000 years. The rate took a sharp upward leap with the invention of writing, but even so it remained painfully slow over centuries of time. The next great leap forward in knowledge acquisition didn't occur until the fifteenth century when Gutenberg and others discovered movable type. Prior to 1500, Europe was producing books at a rate of 1,000 titles per year. By 1950, four and one half centuries later, Europe was producing 128,000 titles per year. What once took a century now took only ten months. By 1960, only a single decade later, the rate had made another significant jump, so that a century's work could be completed in seven and a half months. And by the mid-sixties, the output of books on a world scale, Europe included, approached 1,000 titles per day.*

*While you cannot argue that every book is a net gain for the advancement of knowledge, nevertheless we find that the accelerative curve in book publications does in fact crudely parallel the rate at which man discovered new knowledge. There is reason to believe that the rate is still rising sharply.*

*"What has been learned in the last three decades about the nature of living beings dwarfs in extent of knowledge any comparable period of scientific discovery in the history of mankind, according to biochemist Philip Siekevitz.*

— FUTURE SHOCK
By Alvin Toffler

# How to effectively read materials that are of different styles.

## Novels are not read in the same manner as technical reports.

# Business correspondence.

[1] **Purpose of correspondence.**
— To transmit information.
— To ask for reaction.
— To motivate action.

[2] **Organizational structure of material.**
— Opening and closing paragraphs are usually superficial.
— Mid-section contains the essential information requiring a decision or response.

[3] **How to read business correspondence.**
*Pre-view rapidly, looking for:*
— Who's writing it.
— What he wants.
— What his point of view or attitude is.
— What your response might be.
*Read the material:*
— Concentrate on mid-section for answers to pre-viewed questions. Slow down if you have to here.
— Ignore paragraph sequence. Often paragraphs in business correspondence

are not ordered towards making a point. Don't depend on them for understanding of content. Read each one for individual meaning.

— Condense sentences for meaning. Complicated phrasing, jargon, and the general form often confuse the simple meaning behind them. Translate for the crux of the message as you go. Concentrate on finding the point of the correspondence.

*Mentally recall essentials* of correspondence — are your scanning questions answered? *Re-scan* if necessary to clear up any confusion. Complex, long or disorganized correspondence may require re-scanning.

*Respond.* Decide what to do about correspondence and do it. Write back, telephone, send a telegram, file for reference, etc. Note your decision on the original correspondence for you and/or your secretary's reference.

**Remember to use underlining on *all* reading materials.**

# Technical reports.

Don't let the sometimes forbidding appearance of a technical report frighten you away — these pieces of writing are usually the most well-organized of all reading material. The words can be looked up in various sources if the terminology is unfamiliar to you. The title, structure, headlines, opening and closing sections and diagrams and graphs all give clearly defined information. Use your scanning time to determine how you will use the information — or if you will even need to read it carefully at all. In some cases, only a scanning is necessary for your needs. In other cases, you might want to read and construct detailed mandala notes. React to the material after you read it. Ask yourself questions. Integrate the information with what you already know and allow yourself to see if the material suggests new reading directions to you.

**Remember to use underlining on *all* reading materials.**

# Reading scientific or technical materials.

There is generally an "abstract" at the beginning of the article in a scientific journal. This abstract, which is usually complete in itself, summarizes the entire reading, and is a preview of the purpose and content of the article. When you look at the article, you should see an introduction of one or more paragraphs. This introduction establishes the boundaries of the material, states which way it will be approached and with what type of language, and, finally, the overall organization of the article will be stated.

Conclusions based on the evidence will usually follow, and then will be expanded upon in the main body of the material.

The final paragraphs summarize and offer conclusions and recommendations. Further information which might be useful to someone specializing in the area covered by the article will be placed in the appendices. Acknowledgements are made here, or in a footnote to the title.

**How to approach this type of reading.**

*Scan,* checking title, author, footnotes (see if they give further information or if they are indications of source material), graphs, charts, illustrations, etc.

*Scan again* paying special attention to the abstract, opening paragraphs and large type headings. Then make note, mentally or with a pencil, of the sections most important to you for *your* purpose in reading.

*Now read,* using underlining, varying your speed according to the needs you have set yourself from this material — slow down for important passages. Rescan if necessary. It is now your choice as to whether you want to recall this material mentally, verbally or with a mandala.

# Newspapers.

[1] **Kinds of newspaper writing.**

*News stories* — short, factual reports of the day's events. Very little, if any, interpretation or opinion by writer. Written by newspaper staff or transmitted by various national news services to newspapers around the country who then have the option of printing it.

*Editorials* — comments or opinion on newsworthy events by editorial staff. Point of view usually represents owners of the newspaper.

*Syndicated columns* — short pieces by nationally known writers printed in hundreds of newspapers each day. Personal opinion and view of currently newsworthy topics. Often do not correspond to political policies or opinions of newspapers.

*Advertising* — simply designed to sell products to consumer. Usually labeled "advertisement."

[2] **Organizational structure of newspaper writing.**

*News stories:*

— *Headlines:* The grabber. Gives essence of story.

— *First paragraph:* Covers the who, why, what, where, when and how of story in short, concise sentences.

— *Remainder of article:* each paragraph elaborates on details presented in first paragraph. Explanations, incidents, further information are added in order of importance to the main event. Paragraphs near the end of the article can then be eliminated if space is needed for other articles.

**Editorials:**
— *First paragraph:* usually contains a statement of events or situation on which writer will comment.
— *Mid-section:* the writer's discussion and opinion of the topic.
— *End:* summation of issues and writer's opinion.

**Syndicated columns** — similar to editorials but usually more elaborate.

**Features** — similar to magazine articles. Situations or events to be discussed are stated in the opening paragraphs. The mid-section elaborates, giving facts, incidents, situations and the writer's opinion relating to the main topic. Final paragraphs sum up.

**Advertising** — short or long. Designed to make you believe you can't live without the product.

[3] **How to read a newspaper.**
— Use your scan reading and re-scanning methods. Be especially aware of your background knowledge and/or opinion. Decide how you are going to use the information before you start reading.
— Use your mental, oral or written recall method, depending on the use you've decided to make of the information.
— Be aware of the type of article you are reading:
    Simple factual reporting;
    Opinionated writing;
    Editorial;
— Analyze according to other sources and/or your background knowledge or opinion.
— Vary your reading speed according to length, type of article and what you want to get out of it.
— Read column by column, page by page.

# Typical format of magazine and journal articles

[1] **Type of material**
   — short, prose composition.
   — usually 2500-5000 Words.

[2] **Purpose of material**
   *To quickly and imaginatively inform reader on various topics such as:*
   — a personal experience.
   — a situation.
   — self-help technique.
   — a profile of a person or a group.
   — travel.
   — opinion articles on trends, music, art, etc.

[3] **Kinds of magazines and journals**
   *General interest* (something in it for everyone)
   — Time
   — Esquire
   — Reader's Digest
   *Special interest* (directed towards a particular subject or audience)
   — Today's Health
   — Parents Magazine
   — Scientific American
   — Popular Mechanics
   *Very special interest*
   — Trade journals
   — House organs (publications within companies for employees, organization publications for members, etc.
   — Technical and professional journals

**[4] Organizational structure of material.**

*Simple.*

— similar to newspaper article, often longer

— Opening paragraph: identifies topic, grabs reader's attention

— Remainder of article: reports and discusses items of interest in order of importance to main topic

*Elaborate.*

— Opening paragraph: grabs reader's attention. May not fully identify topic

— Second paragraph: gives author's point of view and his intention to comment

— Main text: facts, observations, situations plus comments by author which reveal his point of view

— Summary: end of article, summarizing quickly the content of article and author's point of view

**[5] How to read magazine and journal articles.**

— Look for attention grabbers in first paragraph.

— Look for essence of article and/or author's point of view in second paragraph.

— Look for facts and explanations in the main body of article.

— Look for summary near the end of the article.

— Use hand movement, recall method and speed appropriate to your intended use of material.

Remember to use underlining on *all* reading materials.

# Novels.

A novel is an *invented* story, fabricating people and situations in an environment of the author's choosing. It is designed to give the author's interpretation of the meaning of people's actions and the situation in which they act.

[1] **Kinds of novels.**

Novels can be very short or very long. They can be set in the past (historical novels), in the present, or in the future (science fiction). They can be written from the first person point of view, ("I") or the third person point of view, ("he" or "she"), or the second person, ("you"), for that matter.

[2] **Purpose of the novel.**

To allow the reader an understanding of events, situations and people the author thinks important. Often a novel simply reveals "what happened," but more often an author attempts to explain, in symbolic terms, through his particular characters and environment, the meaning of some universal situation, common to all human society.

[3] **Structure of the novel.**

— *Description;* narrative, which describes events, situations, and happenings in which the characters move and react. The scene.

— *Character Revelation:* dialogue and description through which the author reveals what kind of people his characters are, how they relate to each other and to the scene in which he has placed them.

**Remember to use underlining on** *all* **reading materials.**

**How to read a novel.**

*Plan to finish a book in one or two sessions.*

This keeps you in touch with the mood and the details, with the unity of the book.

*Decide your methods.*

Use your scanning, reading and re-scanning recall skills. Choose your methods and your reading speed according to how you will use the material (for personal enjoyment, sharing with a friend, learning more about a situation of interest to you, studying for an exam, etc.). Be sure to use paper clips or rubberbands to section off chapters you wish to read as a unit.

*Read the title,* think about it.

Titles are indications of the essential meaning the author wants to convey. Ask yourself why he might have chosen it; pay attention to the images and impressions it creates in your mind before you begin reading.

*Get to know the characters,* as you would new people in your life.

Listen to their conversations, watch how they react in situations. Mentally or in writing, note your impressions of them. Watch to see if they act realistically, either as you yourself expect people to act or in terms of the people and situations in which the author has placed them.

*Be aware of the overall scene* in which the characters are moving.

Keep a sense of the general environment in mind. A broader view of detail will enhance overall understanding.

*What's the author trying to say.*

This is a piece of fantasy, put together by the author's imagination. Very often authors don't write novels just to entertain us. They are frequently commenting on something of universal interest, trying to make their own point about a commonly experienced situation. Think about the deeper meanings of what you're reading as you go along. Often authors use their invented situations and people to symbolize large, universal situations. Think about these possibilities as you go along. Your ability to do this might depend on your background and the knowledge you bring with you to the book. Reading a few novels dealing with the same general situation can be very helpful in enlarging your perspective and your enjoyment.

*Re-scan through the chapter or entire book again after you finish reading.*

*Re-acquaint yourself with the plot, your knowledge of the characters.*

*Think about what happened, see the chapter or book as a whole. Record your impressions and understanding. Repeat again if you feel foggy about something. This is particularly helpful if the book is very long.*

# Short stories.

*The four major forms of fiction are novels* (over 30,000 words), *novelettes* (10,000 words to 30,000 words), *short stories* (2,000 to 10,000 words), and *very short stories* (500 to 2,000 words). The form of a short story is much different from that of a novel, and it is not length alone that makes the difference. Short stories have fewer characters than novels, and more simplicity of plot and characterization. The plot is more direct and compact in a short story. In a novel, there is a more leisurely and detailed style.

When scanning any work of fiction, look first to see if the paragraphs are more dialogue or narrative; sense the mood; check the language and look for basic story elements — characters, time, place. You will usually find it easier to construct a mandala for each sub-section of the story. But your original star mandala should be your first reference point, since it assembles all of the basics of the story into one form.

# POETRY

Poetry is concise and dense — a few words to mean a lot. Poems are not read the same way in which you'd read a newspaper. All poems are meant to be savoured. They can be intellectual, emotional, didactic or propagandistic, but they are always imaginative. Longfellow's "Midnight Ride of Paul Revere" is all those things. Though a long poem, it creates almost as much imagery as a novel, and being written in a narrative style, it reads faster than a poem by T.S. Eliot, for example. Most poems are written to be heard, and poets arrange their lines and stanzas so that they will be read correctly. Other poems, like many of those by E.E. Cummings, are meant to be read, and they are arranged on the page in such a way as to enhance the poem itself. Poems are meant to touch you, to move you, and they can do that only if you are still. Read poetry when you are free of distractions. Poetry is a craft, full of subtleties and surprises. Enjoy.

# What's the use of poetry?

— "What's the Use of Poetry?" by Charlton Ogburn,
reprinted by permission of Readers' Digest.

*Committed to memory,
it can be a solace, a joy, an
inspiration — a resource to last
a lifetime*

For days we had been pressing through the forest of northern Burma to relieve a sister battalion surrounded by the Japanese. As we came out into an open rice field, I looked down the column at the drained, pale faces of the men who make the assault. I marveled at their courage. Ahead we could hear the artillery. That always brought out the craven in me. But to help give me heart I had in my memory William Ernest Henley's lines about a remnant of the Confederate Army:

> *Rags and tatters, belts and bayonets,*
> *On they swung, the drum a-rolling,*
> *Mum and sour. It looked like fighting,*
> *And they meant it, too, by thunder!*

"Romance," the poem is called, and it begins, "Talk of pluck!" Later, 35 years after World War II, I came upon the text from which I had learned the poem. Yellowed with age, it had been typed by my mother, who sent it to me when I was 14 and working on a farm. She sent me many poems, including another by Henley, which, set to music, is known as "Invictus." It begins:

> *Out of the night that covers me,*
> *Black as the Pit from pole to pole,*
> *I thank whatever gods may be*
> *For my unconquerable soul.*

An unconquerable soul was not a thing that, even, at my most euphoric, I could claim. But I was to know times when it took my courage up a notch to recite to myself:

> *Under the bludgeonings of chance,*
> *My head is bloody, but unbowed.*

Hardly written about *me!* Still ...

I mostly memorized the poems my mother copied for me while riding a hayrake, holding the reins of the chestnut mare, round and round the new-mown field in the timeless hours of summer. I could recognize the truth of Keat's lines:

> *The poetry of earth is never dead;*
> *When all the birds are faint with the hot sun*
> *And hide in cooling trees, a voice will run*
> *From hedge to hedge about the new-mown mead.*

In this setting, too, I learned of the flower Tennyson held

> *... root and all, in my hand,*
> *Little flower — but if I could understand*
> *What you are, root and all, and all in all,*
> *I should know what God and man is.*

The eternal, fathomless mystery of creation spoke from these lines. I also read William Blake's declaration that "To see a world in a grain of sand" is to "Hold infinity in the palm of your hand." The truth was so clear I was sure I must have known it all along. Yet without Tennyson and Blake, how long would it have taken me to know I knew it?

In his book *A Study of Poetry*, Bliss Perry, a college professor of mine, wrote of poetry's capacity "for turning fact into truth" and "for lifting the mind, bowed down by wearying thought and haunting fear, into a brooding ecstasy." Perry wrote, as well, of poetry's capacity "for remolding the broken syllables of human speech into sheer music." That is why, early in life, we are susceptible to the verse of Edgar Allan Poe — because of its music, enhanced by an other-worldly mood:

> *The skies they were ashen and sober;*
> *The leaves they were crisped and sere -*
> *The leaves they were withering and sere:*
> *It was night, in the lonesome October*
> *Of my most immemorial year;*
> *It was hard by the dim lake of Auber,*
> *In the misty mid region of Weir;*
> *It was down by the dank tarn of Auber,*
> *In the ghoul-haunted woodland of Weir.*

Those lines became ineradicable in my memory in college. What much of "Ulalume" meant I could not have said — still cannot. But what did it matter, with mesmerizing lines like "ghoul-haunted woodland of Weir"?

For me, a poem has to cry out to be memorized. Like this one:

> O Western wind, when wilt thou blow,
> That the small rain down can rain?
> Christ, that my love were in my arms
> And I in my bed again!

Could yearning be more poignantly evoked than in those lines, which sprang from a nameless English heart nearly five centuries ago?

It is only when we memorize poetry that we truly possess it, and it us. My mother spent the last two years of her life bedridden. Her sight had so far left her that she could no longer read. Her hearing soon followed. Now poetry came to her rescue.

In high school Mother had been taught to memorize familiar staples of poetry, and she knew how young Lochinvar came out of the west, what the ancient Mariner told the Wedding Guest and where the wigwam of Nokomis stood (by the shores of Gitchee Gumee). But all roads led her in time to Shakespeare. She could recite his sonnets by the dozen, among them Sonnet 30, which voices the heartache we all must know toward the end:

> When to the sessions of sweet silent thought
> I summon up remembrance of things past,
> I sign the lack of many a thing I sought,
> And with old woes new wail my dear time's waste.

All of us, at times every day, are thrown upon our own mental resources and are fortunate if among them are poems we can play over to ourselves. To do this is to know the gratifications a musician experiences in performing the work of a master.

If poetry we know by heart can add so to our lives, should memorizing it not have a wider appeal?

Many of us who would enjoy having poetry committed to memory are put off by the seeming effort it requires. We need not be. A habit of reading poetry grows upon one, and there is no need to force ourselves back to well-loved poems. It is not long before we have them half memorized. For my part, I find I soon have the rest if I write the lines on slips of paper I can put in a pocket and take out while waiting at a traffic light, walking or in an elevator.

Poetry made our own can do wonders for our powers of expression. It can match and intensify our moods, and strengthen our aspirations. Even the poetry of despondency can help us, as Malcolm in Shakespeare's *Macbeth* urges:

> *Give sorrow words: the grief that does not speak*
> *Whispers the o'er-fraught heart, and bids it break.*

Great poetry, if we have it in our hearts, can help us — as Kipling enjoins — to

> *. . . meet with Triumph and Disaster*
> *And treat those two impostors just the same.*

As Lord Byron puts it in "To Thomas Moore":

> *Here's a sigh to those who love me,*
> *And a smile to those who hate;*
> *And, whatever sky's above me,*
> *Here's a heart for every fate.*

ALPINE PHLOX

# *Step V*

## *Decisions & Memory*

. . . our mysterious and often misunderstood memories

# Decisions & Memory.

## *The Lost Arts of Memory*

*Before the printed book, Memory ruled daily life and the occult learning and fully deserved the name later applied to printing, the "art preservative of all arts" (Ars artium omnium conservatrix). The Memory of individuals and of communities carried knowledge through time and space. For millennia personal Memory reigned over entertainment and information, over the perpetuation and perfection of crafts, the practice of commerce, the conduct of professions. By Memory and in Memory the fruits of education were garnered, preserved, and stored. Memory was an awesome faculty which everyone had to cultivate, in ways and for reasons we have long since forgotten. In these last five hundred years we see only pitiful relics of the empire and the power of Memory.*

— THE DISCOVERERS
By Daniel J. Boorstin

# Decisions & Memory.

*You must:*

[1] ***Decide* exactly what you are going to do with the information you are about to read.** What do you want to get from reading this material? Is there an interest you want to satisfy? Try to be selective about what you want to remember.

[2] ***Trust* your memory and have confidence in your ability to remember.** Never let a negative attitude interfere with your reading process.

[3] ***Grasp* a subject or theme from the chapter or article you are reading and develop a way you want to look at it *for your own needs*.** Try to see what the main issue or point of the book or article is. Then develop a mental "set" or point of view towards the article you will be reading. Consider your previous knowledge on this subject and your reflections upon it.

[4] ***Read* with an *intention* to stimulate your own thinking and ideas.** Prepare your own mind to respond on all levels — interest, curiosity, emotional involvement. Do you know why you chose to read this book or article? Keep it in mind at all stages in the reading process.

[5] ***Do something active* with the material.** The fifth step is one of the most important parts of reading with purpose. Why? Well, experiments have shown that people usually remember more accurately when they have something active to do with 'just read' material. **There are three ways to do this.**

**There are three ways to do this.**

> *Mental* — by repeating material to yourself, in your mind.

> *Verbal* — by telling someone about what you have read.

> *Written* — by writing notes down about what you have read.

Each of these methods will improve your ability to recall reading material. But **the most effective and lasting method** is the third — **written recall**. The mandala memory system of our manual discusses this third method and introduces to you a totally new system of note-taking. *(See page 96.)*

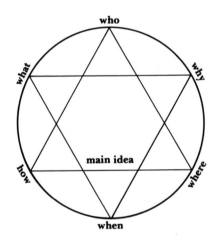

# Why do we forget?

Let's examine the basic mechanism responsible for forgetting. The **seeming impairment** of memory is not a disturbance in the function of memory but rather a **symptom** of deeper unconscious "memory blocks" which interfere with the normal and natural use of your memory banks. [See left.]

All people have unwittingly crippled their phenomenal natural capacity to remember.

*These memory blocks may vary in degree with each individual but will always consist of a combination of the following conditions:*
**Negative early training causing nervousness, anxiety, fear, tension, grief, anger and depression, fatigue, poor nutrition, alcohol, hunger and natural body changes.**

### A 'poor memory' is merely a poorly used memory!

Have you ever heard of Sodium Pentothal? Well, it's a truth serum which is injected into your bloodstream and affects your system in many of the same ways that hypnosis does. If you are asked any questions about the past your memory blocks will be "short-circuited" and you will be able to answer. The answer is always correct, because with no conscious blocks your *perfect memory* is accessible. It always works. But then if you believe that there was some extraordinary effort involved, think again! The drug (or hypnosis) relax your body and mind, and there cannot be an avoidance such as "I can't remember," or "I have a bad memory," or some other subconscious judgement.

So! now you see *the reality of perfect memory*. It's there! *It has always been there! It will always be there!*

If an artifical stimulus can bring up memories long buried, then it stands to reason the memory was there to begin with. Hypnosis or

Sodium Pentothal merely urge **existent information** to the surface. They do not create information. **Memories already exist** but are filed away awaiting your orders to re-surface. When you say to yourself or utter aloud such things as, "I can't remember" or "I have a bad memory," you are, in fact, giving an order to the memory bank to keep the material buried in the sub-conscious instead of giving an inner command that is positive.

**Does this sound familiar?**

"I can't get up this morning," or "Boy, am I clumsy," or "I'm just not the type to jog," (even though the doctor has just informed you that you're dangerously over-weight and smoke too much and exercise too little and might die if you don't do something soon!)

Well, my friend, you can be clumsy, you can sleep your life away and you can die, *or,* you can start by **thinking differently** — *now, right this minute!*

*A major reason we seem unable to do certain things is simply because we have become comfortable with negative images of our minds and our body's capabilities. These images can be easily changed, but you will have to* **pay your dues**. What I mean by that is, find out HOW you can change and then DO whatever you have to do in order to become the **powerful**, **wonderful**, **intelligent person** you were meant to be!

An excellent way to start is by reading this text, and trying out all suggestions and exercises, thereby actualizing more of your *real potential*.

*Francis Bacon told us that "Knowledge is power." This can now be translated into contemporary terms. In our social setting, "Knowledge is change." And accelerating knowledge acquisition, fueling the great engine of technology, means accelerating change.*

— **Future Shock**
By Alvin Toffler

# Commands and control.

If you want to increase your memory power, you must **vow never** to utter the preceding negative statements again! Make a conscious effort NOW to **use only positive statements** such as "I'm sure I can remember, just give me a moment." Then, say to yourself, something like, "Mind, work for me now, work for me now, work for me NOW." Do not stir or go on until the requested memory comes to you, then, write it down and look directly at it to validate the fact that your very command triggered a REAL RESPONSE. One validation turns a key in the understanding of your own thinking capabilities. It is pleasurable. It will give you the feeling of being in control. As humans respond to pleasure by wanting to repeat the action that initiated the feeling, commanding your mind to respond more often will be the outcome. The more you command your mind and memory to work at YOUR COMMAND, the more it will respond. I liken this to the development of muscle, in that, the more you use your muscles, the more you **are able** to use your muscles.

## Awareness and Belief.

**From the moment of your conception and birth your memory has been perfect.**

**Why** do you think you don't use all your memory power? **Why** do you suppose you aren't using or exercising this limitless memory power? **Why** is it "common knowledge" that only a chosen few have perfect memories? Why are there only a handful of people called 'geniuses'?

It's because you are basically unaware of the perfect memory you possess RIGHT NOW!

My course UNLOCKS your perfect memory, allowing the inborn powers of your mind to work for you. There is no overt effort needed in order to make your memory work. It only takes two small things.

[1] **First, you must BE AWARE that you have a perfect memory.**

[2] **Second, you must BELIEVE that you have a perfect memory!**

Your memory is always perfect in every way. Always **instantly available**, ever present, and always TOTAL. The countless habitual acts you perform daily prove that you are using perfect memory every moment that you breathe.

Why in the world would you not use these powers? **Habit** is one reason. Humans become very locked into and comfortable with habit, whether harmful or not, because humans tend to be afraid of change. That's the magic word, my friend, *"CHANGE (not pain) is how to gain!"*

Believe what you read. Try all the exercises. Don't skip details. Then enrich your life with these simple formulas for the successful release of your mental powers.

*It is hard to define and clarify intelligence: intelligence tests themselves are actually tests of experience and manipulation, the use of language, the ability to relate to a commonly perceived set of symbols, the ability to see a common cultural configuration. What we test and recognize is limited by the questions we can devise and our ability to conceive of a system in which those questions ae meaningful.*

*Intelligence can be described as awareness.*
— Mind In The Waters
Assembled by Joan McIntyre

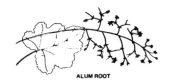

ALUM ROOT

I will attempt to make it known to you just "why" you forget, and then, when you see this dangerous and bad habit, you will be able to more intelligently decide whether you want to continue using it or discard it. The decision is yours, but once you have heard or read that your mind is a perfect record of all detail ever encountered, you can never pretend to *not* know. Once you know that your mind is perfect in every way and that your memory works on command, you can never again say, "I can't remember." If the thought escapes you momentarily, you can say, "It'll come to me in a moment," or, "I'll try and keep trying."

# The Functions and Mechanics of Memory

# Our Mysterious and Often Misunderstood Memory

## The Functions and Mechanics of Memory

### Thinking differently about the nature of memory and mind power, is 'the KEY.'

When you perceive that remembering is a physical activity rather than a cerebral **event**, **every last vestige of mystery** concerning memory disappears. And then you *are thinking differently* about it.

The simple truth about memory is so fundamentally basic it has eluded our grasp since the beginning of time. The Big Secret of recall is that your subconscious mind continuously records and remembers every experience **permanently** and **perfectly**.

The natural activities of your mind are the endless processing of memories and experiences. Your mind can never stop recording, even during sleep. Memories are made and stored in your subconscious without effort, without desire or need. The mind records automatically and continuously with perfection, and this minute detail can be recalled years later with the same perfection.

Hypnosis has many case histories that prove this point. Our libraries are full of scientific data that refers to the recalling of information long stored in the subconscious. The solving of crimes by police has had a 'shot in the arm' since doctors have incorporated hypnotic techniques for getting crime victims and witnesses to recall information forgotten through fear and shock. Sodium Pentothal has been widely used to extract detail forgotten or stored. Why am I telling you this? Well, it is further proof that memories are stored, and even when an artificial stimulus is used, the mind reacts to this stimulus by divulging the requested information. **In simpler terms, to recall something stored in the subconscious, one need only *demand* that the information be released for use!** ("Ask and you shall receive.")

**[For further proof of this release, try the exercise on the next page, but carefully follow the instructions.]**

## Instructions:

1. Stare at the center of the diagram for one full minute. [See next page.]
2. Blink your eyes.
3. Stare at the blank page until you see the image of the star-burst.
4. See if you can reproduce the image on the wall or ceiling.

*Please use Exercise A. on the next page.*

Exercise A.

## So, my friend . . .

Did you have to struggle in order to re-create the star-burst? Was it painful? *I think not!* That is, if you followed my instructions exactly. Did you see the image in colors (usually pastels)? Did the image appear larger or smaller? (Sometimes it will.) Most of my students experience a sensation of joy and amazement or amusement.

Think of it! Just now you gave yourself a simple command, and the command triggered a wonderful response. Each time you give yourself a command that is positive, a feeling of well being will replace, little by little, your feelings of having a memory that is seemingly inadequate. **Remember, "a poorly used memory," is exactly THAT!**

*Call on your own memory. Work it. Play games that challenge your memory. (Many are suggested in this text.) Remember,* **the more you use your mind for recall, the more you will be able to use your mind.** Makes sense, doesn't it?

## Knowing, then believing.

You do not have to rehearse or force an incident or an impression on your mind in order to remember it. Every impression is automatically photographed and retained or preserved even if you are not consciously aware of it:

*"It is estimated that in one lifetime, a brain can store 1,000,000,000,000,000 (a million billion) bits of information."*

— THE HUMAN BRAIN
By Isaac Asimov

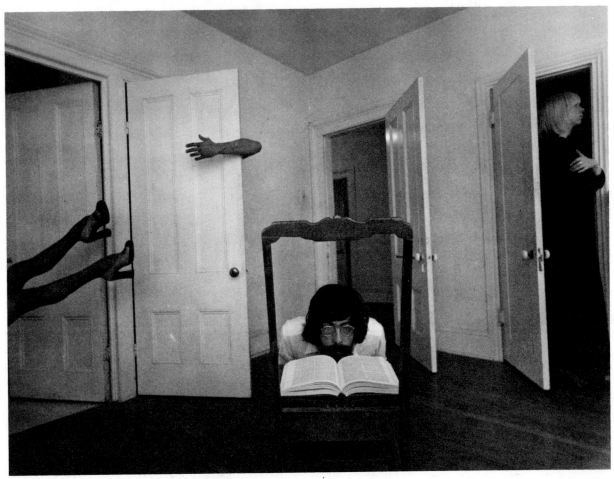

—Ron Thal

Every scene your eyes take in, every sound you hear, every feeling you perceive, every emotion you experience, every taste you delight in or shrink from, every scent you pick up and much, much more is faultlessly recorded and stored by your subconscious right from the beginning of your life. One million billion bits of information are continuously processed during your lifetime.

When you understand this wonderful capacity of your brain, you can then work on its development. Not a moment before!

# Inner workings of the mind.

**We tend to forget things *not* because our memories are faulty but because we are fundamentally unaware of the inner workings and mechanics of our own mental machine.**

I do not think that you would get into a car and take off down a highway knowing only that one pedal was for GOING and the other for STOPPING! Think of the trouble you would immediately be in. Think of the danger.

**Now, how much do you really know about the workings of your inner machine, the mind? Why do you suppose we have breakdowns and traumas, and mental as well as physical problems?**

The experts say, "Most disease, whether mental or physical, is MOSTLY IN THE MIND and can be controlled with a change in mental attitude." Sure sounds easy doesn't it? The truth is, we have been brought up to believe that if there is no pain, there is no gain, and somehow all the drilling from parents, teachers, friends and relations has convinced us that the 'pain-gain' relationship is real. As a knowledgeable person on the subject, and after using the last seventeen years of my life searching for answers about 'mind power', I have found that pain and strife are not the only way to enlightenment. Francis Bacon once said, "Knowledge *is* power." Most memory experts agree and go on to say that knowing facts about mind power and memory and then **BELIEVING** coupled with the exercise of that belief triggers something psychologically that

**permits the USE** of more of our mental capabilities.

Think of it! Once you know a thing, you then can begin using that knowledge.

**Sounds too easy, doesn't it?** Consider this, my friend. Let's go back to the engine of a car and the mechanics of driving safely and competently down the highway. Once you know that a red light means STOP, how often are you going to go through one and endanger your loved ones? A simple fact. An acknowledged simple action.

The parallel here is simple and clean. The more you are aware of the inner workings of perfect thinking and perfect memory, the more you will tend to exercise these workings.

# The miracle of life called memory.

*Many people, I among them, believe that you and I are walking funds of information, carrying all the memories accumulated **not only during your lifetime, but also the inherited memories of the entire race accumulated since the beginning of time.***

*You do not **have** to know why your mind works, it just does! But understanding will help you make it work better.*

# Your Inner Truth

Because of early training, most of the population turns a deaf ear, so to speak, to the real truths about memory and awareness. You will notice during the course of this book that I repeat myself on all issues many times and in different ways. Why is it that I must put myself to this task? Well, negative statements such as, "I had a friend once who was considered a genius" or "I heard one time that there was a teacher in Chicago with a photographic mind" are heard every day. Such statements reinforce the erroneous notion that there are only a handful of these "special" persons alive today.

This common belief can be found almost everywhere. With a student along, I walked into a bakery in my hometown and asked a simple question of a friend who was also there, "Betty, do you know of any persons who are true geniuses?" Betty answered right off the top of her head, "Wasn't Abraham Lincoln supposed to be that way?" That day, my student got the picture.

After many such encounters, this young student shook her head and said that before I had showed her the inner truth about her abilities, she too had thought the same thing.

The point is, **if you continue to believe incorrect ideas, they will remain firm, and in fact, create within your subconscious a suppression of your own genius.**

Once you know the inner truth, the fact of your own real genius, and the potential of your own real mind power, you will then be able to release that genius by the power of your will alone.

Power your thoughts with the truth about their capabilities. One such truth is that our mental powers are virtually untapped. We only use a small portion of the brain power we possess. Most of us still do not consciously use both hemispheres of our brains even though it is widely known that it is not only possible but that there are those of us right now who have been tested and do use both hemispheres.

The techniques in this course are well-developed from the knowledge gained through research exploring the minds and actions of geniuses, achievers with "photographic" minds, and naturally fast readers who retain 80-90% of all they read.

By following this course information and the accompanying exercises, you will begin a natural process (long suppressed) of experiencing the joy and wonder of your own mind power. You will first learn the Mechanics of Memory and then the Power of Inner Commands.

My grandfather once said, "Once you know the truth you are no longer free." Now that you know how your mind works, **you are no longer free to say that you "cannot remember!"** If you continue not to remember things that happen or items you read, you can only say, "I choose not to remember." (But, then, who would do such a thing?) **Knowledge is survival.**

*You Are What You Think.*
*You Are The Product Of Your Thoughts.*

# Your Mental Storehouse

As they occur, your mind is accurately keeping a record of every sensory incident at all times, whether you are awake or asleep. Your mind, right now, is the most perfect information center on earth. You do not **use** all your powers of mind because up until now you have been **unaware** of your mental capabilities. No other reason exists.

Depth analysis, hypnosis, and truth serums demonstrate that you were born with a perfect memory. You alone are in command of the direction in which your personal powers of mind are exercised. If you do not use those powers wisely, you will lose them.

Have you ever attended a football or baseball game, or concerts where literally thousands of people are screaming and jumping while something wondrous is going on onstage or in the field? Have you noticed how you can pick a face in the crowd or the sound of a voice you recognize over and above the deafening sound of the other people?

Have you ever gone to a museum and in a flash of an instant chosen a painting you like more than all the rest? When viewing such a painting, did you see the whole painting? Ask yourself the following questions. Was I aware of the temperature of the room? Was I aware of hunger or any other need? Did I simultaneously accept or reject the painting? Most people can answer yes to all the above questions. You're probably wondering, "Why all these questions?"

One point I want to make crystal clear to you,

dear student, is that your body and mind are so exquisitely capable that thousands of incidents per second are happening all around you all the time and are recorded and stored instantaneously and perfectly, which is further proof of the real potential within your mind.

On page 198 is the Inner Commmand Technique that will work for you every time you care to use it. First, though, you must learn and practice this command until it becomes comfortable and a part of you.

## New changes.

There is a small price you must pay in order to change your thinking about the possibilities of brain power. You must consciously **desire** to know how to utilize your magnificant mental abilities, and then, you must **decide** to use the information.

I can just imagine you now, dear student, you're probably staring at that last paragraph and thinking, "Sure, that sounds easy to her, but all my life I've had a problem remembering names, facts, numbers, my mother's maiden name, not to mention anniversaries, birthdays, and so forth. Can it really be that simple?"

You have nothing to lose. Try relaxing and then just daydream about having a perfect memory. Dream about all the things you would love to study or read but until now have been afraid of. Dream of the joy you might feel when you recall every detail of that journal you must read for your job. Then look in the mirror and say firmly and audibly, "**My mind is perfect, and I am in control at all times. My memory will work perfectly for me upon command every time I call upon it. I am and have always** been a child of the universe, no less than the trees and stars, and I have a right to be here."

The above exercise used each night before bed and each morning upon awakening will enable you to enrich your mental powers and physical abilities a thousand fold. In the beginning, make sure you use this command at the same time each day and night to establish a pattern. Until now, dear student, you have been establishing your negative outlook on mental power for your entire life. **So give yourself a fighting chance at changing your way of thinking**, because that's what it will take.

## Knowing the difference.

Only when you know the "why" of a thing can you make an intelligent decision on how to judge it or make it work for you.

I will attempt to make you understand just why you forget, and then when you see this dangerous and bad habit, you will then be able to decide more intelligently whether you want to continue using it or discard it. The decision is yours, but once you have heard or read that your mind is a perfect record of all detail ever encountered, you can never pretend to not 'know'. Once you know that your mind is perfect in every way and that your memory works on command, you can never again say, "I can't remember." If the thought escapes you momentarily, you can say, "It'll come to me in a moment" or "I'll try and keep trying."

The very exercise of changing your statement starts a spark of electricity and energy to your memory banks enabling you, more and more, to use your storehouse of information. The **Power of Positive Thinking** is the single most energizing ability of the brain known to us. Never say, "I can't!" Say instead, "I'll try."

Forget your negative past. Even in the most barren places, perfect wildflowers will grow.

## How, not what.

I have endeavored to teach my students how to think, not what to think. All of them, no matter what their age, or educational backgrounds, have responded by releasing their inherent creative potential.

Daydreaming is the creative thrust of the brain when not supplied with enough stimula. In test after test, humans **choose** to create.

## Your own uniqueness.

It's been my experience that the mind can easily become bored: hence, daydreams. I believe this dreaming during class or lectures or company meetings is your brain giving you the signals of higher intelligence. Your mind is so complex and capable to begin with that you can call on it anytime you wish and it will respond in whatever ways you command.

Learn these new commands. The more you do, the more accurate your memory will be. In other words, I am showing you how to make your mind work for you, but **it is up to you**, to decide **what** you want to remember. There will be things you need to remember, things you prefer to forget, things you choose to remember, and things your boss or coach or parents choose for you to remember. It will ultimately be **your choice**, on **what** you remember. You **are** and **have always been** in charge of your own destiny.

Daydreaming is a command given by the subconscious to counter boredom. In other words, if your conscious mind isn't doing its job of providing enough stimulation through external data, the subconscious overrides those circuits and substitutes daydreams.

Daydreaming is the creative thrust of the brain when not supplied with enough stimuli. In test after test, humans **choose** to create.

When your subconscious is in charge, you are out of control. This course was designed to teach you how to be in control more of the time.

*The self image we harbor is the key to the success or failure of our most cherished plans and aspirations. If the image is inadequate (and psychologists say most of us habitually underrate ourselves) it behooves us to correct it. We do this by systematically imagining that we are already the sort of person we wish to be.*

— Psycho-Cybernetics
By Maxwell Maltz

**BUR CLOVER**

*It is now time to learn the inner mechanics and techniques of awareness commands.*

# Awareness commands.

You must fully comprehend that this positive system is used to create in you a habit pattern of constantly breaking through the spell of negative early conditioning about the actual nature and mechanics of mind power.

This course presents the most direct method I have found to recover memories from the subconscious storehouse. These release command techniques will be used to facilitate instant recall of any memory you desire to surface.

These inner directives instruct your mind to reproduce memories automatically and instantaneously at your command. These commands are know as **memory activators** or **memory triggers**. As I have said before, your memory can only be released by a command from you.

**Try this little test**:

> Demand of yourself at this moment to picture
>    Abe Lincoln's face.
> Do you see it now?
> Can you see his face in your mind's eye?
> Most people can, with no trouble, recall Abe's face.

**You have just experienced instant memory with no pain or effort** and this supports my theories of **command/recall**.

On the following pages you will learn the actual techniques and mechanics of the whole process of inner-dialogue for more control of the command system. You will find all techniques natural and not painful or stressful. With everyday practice, in a short time you will be able to call to mind any detail whenever you wish.

The commands should be direct, **positive**, slow and impressive. These commands, or creative directives to your unconscious mind, should be made **mentally**; however, if you are so inclined, they may be spoken. Whether mental or verbal, it is extrememly important that they be given with total confidence and a detached self-assurance. By using logical reasoning, you can now exercise **absolute** confidence that your memory reproduces everything automatically. Feelings of doubt will undermine your use of this naturally great faculty.

# Do you sometimes find it impossible to concentrate?

With all the world's distractions, your work, children, and the problems that plague us all, it's no wonder that concentration is difficult!

Is there any way out?

You bet there is!

**First organize your time, then organize your mind.**

I have taught people to organize their time and habits so that they were able to **"Key-In"** on reading material no matter how busy they were, or how noisy it was around them. "Keying-in" means to lock out distractions, to close the mind to everything except the material one is about to read.

Follow my directions and you will quickly become able to concentrate on anything you wish to read, at a higher level than you've ever thought possible.

My philosophy has always been that we were not put on this earth to be failures, or to die without ever having lived. Purposefulness, happiness and productivity are part of the plan of creation for human beings. Just look at the wildflowers born perfect and beautiful, much as we are, to live and die. Would the Almighty Power wish anything less than perfection for us?

*Accomplishing something is a way of loving yourself; experiencing yourself in a positive way allows you to love yourself. When this occurs, all sorts of wonderful things start happening for you.*

**— A.R.**

This long overdue book on reading excellence contains a plan for you to use throughout your life. Learn the information I have made available to you, then use it and perfect a skill which is truly attainable, totally natural and actually very easy to do — as easy as watching a sunset, lifting your hand, opening your eyes. Many have tried and succeeded to read this way and you owe it to yourself to succeed.

*You are now on the path.*

Unlike the flowers of the field, however, people have much control over their destinies. The flowers are fixed in their environment, while we have the freedom to change our destiny.

# Self-dialogue Technique.

## Command Preparation.

*Please do not skip one word on the next two pages.*

This exercise, in a short period of time, will become part of your everyday ritual. It is so natural that once you learn it, it will make sense to use it for many reasons.

Businessmen and women have told me that, before they attend meetings, or begin the business day, they block out the day's distractions with my thirty-second exercise. Many of my college and high school students use the same exercise before tests or in between classes when they feel too distracted. Some of my younger students have confided that they use this technique when their parents are scolding them.

The exercise itself has a centering effect on the person using it. When a basketball player is shooting a crucial shot, he or she holds very still and becomes very centered before throwing the ball. When a player is off center mentally, the ball will always miss its target. Centering takes practice so give yourself a chance. Read through all the instructions a few times just to get the hang of it, then find your place to begin. **Centering is a means of getting in touch with yourself physically and mentally.** It is an inward balance.

# Preparation.

[1.] Make sure the room in which you are to practice is comfortably warm.

[2.] Do not wear uncomfortable or binding clothes. Loose, pajama-type, comfy garments will be less distracting than tight jeans, for example.

[3.] Take the phone off the hook or practice at a time when you will not be disturbed.

[4.] Allow at least ten FULL minutes for the exercise itself, and another five to ten minutes to reflect on what is happening within your mind and body. Linger awhile to savor the sensations inside your mind. Delight in the experience of being in control. Listen to your inner voice and allow your body to follow each mental comand I am about to teach you.

[5.] Lie on the floor or sit in a chair with your hands on your lap, or stand with your back up against the wall. (Try all three on different days so that you can decide which is more comfortable for you.)

**Take a deep, deep breath and then exhale.** Try again. Take a few more deep breaths. Now inhale, exhale.

**Close your eyes for a moment and breathe deeply again.**

**Go inside your mind and give the command to your toes to tighten up.**

[Study carefully.]

Now, did you notice that your toes obeyed? You didn't have to go down there and grab your toes with your fingers and make them tighten up did you? You gave a mental command and the command carried down to your toes and they obeyed. The command itself was directed immediately to your toes.

All of this has happened before, hasn't it? What I mean is that you have given your body signals before and it has obeyed. Each time you lift your hand to brush away an insect or piece of dust from your face, each time one foot moves ahead of the other, each time you brush your teeth, each time you do any of a million different human things in everyday living, you are putting into practice the command/response techniques. The real miracle is that, a silent command, an invisible thing, can get the desired results. The signal goes out, then the toes tighten.

Now it is time for you to go to the next step and through to all the other commands. Just remember, dear student, concentrate on what is happening to you as a result of the commands. Do not discount the ease with which this will all happen or there will be an override on your comprehension of this command/response technique.

Let's start over now, and this time, complete the entire process without stopping.

**Take several deep breaths. Deep breath again.**

**Now, start with your toes and tighten all of them. Hold it** (keep toes very tight).

**Now the balls of your feet.** Tighten them without letting go of the toes.

**Now the arch of your feet.** Tighten and hold. (Do not release anything.)

**Now tighten the heels of your feet.** Keep holding tight all other componants.

**Now your ankles, tighten and hold.**

**Tighten your lower calves and hold.** Do not let go of anything yet.

**Now tighten your upper calves and hold tight.**

**Now your knees. Hold everything very tight and do not release yet.**

**Now your thighs. Tighten and hold. Now your buttocks and tummy.** Hold very tight. Go on. . . .

Tighten your lower back and feel the command climb to your shoulders and down your arms into your wrists and into your hands and fingers. Tighten and hold.

**Now your neck. Hold and go up to your scalp and down to your facial componants, eyes, cheeks, mouth.**

*Hold everything* **to a count of five. (Slowly)**

**Now, let everything go.** Feel all the anxieties leaving your body. Visualize them leaving your body. Let them go.

Shake your hands and feet and breathe deeply again for a few breaths.

You are now ready. You are now open for any new information or idea. You are now able to understand how your mind can give a non-verbal command and your body responds without error.

*Soon, dear student, you will be able to perform this exercise anytime you wish. (When you are in an elevator, your office, a schoolroom, on a bus, a plane or driving down the highway.)*

*For the first week, however, you mst not try to rush the feelings that will become apparent as you perfect the above technique. As a goal, in this method, you should strive to accustom your conscious mind to giving these commands. In other words, you might have to force yourself to find the same time each day to practice, but it's important that it be the same time each day in order to establish a pattern or habit. The entire exercise will take no more than thirty seconds to a minute. The feelings will last a half hour or more. It is at that time that new material should be read. Your retention of materials read at this time will be much more comprehensive and lasting than it would have been had you not done the exercise.*

*As you perfect my techniques, more and more of the materials you will read, (using all my steps that will lead you to reading excellence), will become more and more available at your will.*

*— Motherly Advice*

# On practice, again.

Now that you are acquainted with the major speed-reading methods, you *must* decide that from now on you will *never* read without using them. Twice a day, sit down in a quiet place and for half an hour, **practice** using your new reading techniques. Remember especially to use hand motions down the page — circular or quest for scanning; underlining with fingers for reading. Choose anything to read that is **easy**. This is very important. Training yourself in new reading techniques, like any other skill, requires simple and easy steps in the beginning. The more complex material will come later. Use a newspaper, a magazine or an easily read novel.
**Another hint to remember:**
Make a promise to yourself about your reading timetable. It really helps! The reason? Well, we are all creatures of habit. To make the most of this, we can create a new habit right now — by practicing at the *same time* every day. If you follow through on my advice, you will strengthen your ability to read.

CREAM CUPS

CALIFORNIA BUTTERCUP

*We are engineered as goal seeking mechanisms, and feel lost unless we have a goal which interests us. Your automatic creative mechanism operates in terms of goals and end results. Once you give it a definite goal to achieve, you can depend upon its automatic guidance system to take you to that goal much better than you ever could by conscious thought. But to accomplish this, the goal must be seen so clearly that it becomes real to your brain and nervous system.*

*Your automatic mechanism cannot tell the difference between an actual experience and one which is vividly imagined. The only information available to it concerning any given situation is what you believe to be true about it.*

— PSYCHO-CYBERNETICS
By Maxwell Maltz

To survive, to avert what we have termed future shock,
the individual must become infinitely more adaptable
and capable than ever before. He must search out
totally new ways to anchor himself, for all the old roots:
religion, nation, community, family or profession, are
shaking under the hurricane impact of the accelerative
thrust.

— **FUTURE SHOCK**
By Alvin Toffler

# Reading with purpose.

How many times have you daydreamed through a page or several pages only to snap to attention and discover that you have no idea of the ground you've covered? That won't happen to you any more if you read with purpose. To be successful sometimes means **to know** what you want to do, **decide how** to do it and then **do it** at the proper time. Knowledge of what you want is called a **goal**. You might say that success is the realization, slow but sure, of some pre-determined goal.

For successful reading, you must also have some goals.

It is totally natural to remember what you read. You must, however, have a destination and a plan when you begin a new book.

If you know **what** you wish to remember, you will certainly remember it. If you know what you want **to do** with the information from the book, you will recall the ideas.

**The desire to do something creates the very thing that you desire.**

But you cannot pick up a book and read it without first being clear in your mind about what you're doing.

***Some words of caution***: **Don't skip steps. Don't add speed too soon.**

If you follow all the steps I have shown you so far, you will develop extraordinary reading powers. But don't skip steps. Keep to the order I have shown you.

Each step is a lesson in the *mechanics* of speed reading. Become comfortable with each lesson before attempting to go to the next step. If you are completely ready for each new dimension of the process, you will become a very strong and confident speed reader. **Don't skip steps**. If you are too hard on yourself and expect too much too soon, **slow down**. Learn a little more about your mind and how it works while reading. Learn a little more about how to handle different types of reading material, how to use different pre-reading methods, how designs can stimulate your memory, how to overcome some common resistances to learning these new skills which I have discovered in my students. Once you are really in control, you can speed up as much as you like and skim over the pages like any racing enthusiast.

[1] **Warm up and key-in.**
[2] **Hold reading material properly.**
[3] **"Section off" area to be read.**
[4] **Underline all titles, subtitles, etc.**
[5] **Scan.**
[6] **Make decisions on how you will use this material.**

SCARLET COLUMBINE

# *Step VI*
## *Play with Words*

*Cold words freeze people, and hot words scorch them, and bitter words make them bitter, and wrathful words make them wrathful. Kind words also produce their own image on men's souls: and a beautiful image it is. They soothe, quiet and comfort the hearer.*

*— Blaise Pascal*

# Word games are fun intellectual pastimes.

FIVE SPOT

*Play is a hallmark of intelligence and is indispensable for creativity and flexibility.*
— MIND IN THE WATERS
Assembled by Joan McIntyre

*Learning through play is an important part of animal and human behavior.*
— THE ACT OF CREATION
By Arthur Koestler

# Of course there's a word for it!

Almost everything has a name, but there are lots of things with names so obscure practically no one except dictionary editors knows them. Thus, we have words like **whatchamacallit**, **thingamabob** and **doohickey** — all purpose words that mean "this little thing here whose name I have temporarily forgotten or maybe never knew and I'll bet you don't either."

But this is copping out. Here, as a public service, are 20 words for things that are all around you. You ought to know what to call 'em.

- **Aglet.** The little plastic tip of your shoelace is an aglet. When your aglet breaks, it's tough to get the end of the lace to go through the hole.

- **Anatomical Snuffbox.** You have two of these. It's the hollow that is formed by the meeting of two tendons at the back of the hand and the base of the thumb.

- **Berm.** When you're digging a hole, you shovel the dirt into a pile next to the hole, right? The space between the pile of dirt and the edge of the hole is the berm. Really.

- **Bollard.** The little post you wind a boat's rope around to tether the boat to the dock is a bollard. The same name is applied to the posts in a row in the supermarket parking lot that are spaced wide enough to walk through but too close to let your shopping cart through.

- **Calk.** Look closely at a horseshoe and you'll see it has small things that stick out on the bottom so the horse won't slip and break a leg. Horses don't know what they're called either. They're called calks.

- **Cissing.** When wet varnish separates into spots and streaks so part of what you're varnishing doesn't get covered at all, that's cissing.

- **Dottle.** If you smoke a pipe, you're familiar with this. It's the half-smoked tobacco you have to keep cleaning out of the bottom of the bowl.

- **Duff.** The decaying leaves, pine needles and weeds all over the ground in the forest. Duff is something like dottle on a large scale, only it usually smells better.

# If you don't know a zarf from a dingbat, maybe you should —

→ **Flews.** In case you never noticed, some dogs have big, heavy flaps on the sides of their mouths, which are often covered with saliva. The flaps are called flews.

➡ **Harp.** That metal thing holding a lampshade on a lamp. Sometimes you have to fiddle with the harp when you change a light bulb.

☞ **Kerf.** The slit you make when you start to saw a piece of wood. As you keep sawing, the kerf gets bigger and bigger until it disappears and you have two pieces of wood.

→ **Kick.** That's the indentation in the bottom of a wine bottle. It's supposed to add strength to the glass. It also makes the bottle look as if it holds more than it does.

➡ **Philtrum.** The vertical indentation in the space above your upper lip. For those with mustaches, it separates the left half from the right. For the rest of us, it doesn't do much at all.

☞ **Schizocarp.** You probably played with schizocarps when you were a kid, but didn't know it. Those winged things from maple trees that you put on your nose and than spin like pinwheels when you toss them into the wind are schizocarps.

→ **Snath.** The handle of a scythe. If you break it, you're in trouble. How would you like to have to call a hardware store and ask, "Do you sell scythe snaths, sir?"

➡ **Snood.** The fleshy growth on a turkey's face that helps make him so ugly. It's hard to look good with a snood on your face.

☞ **Tang.** The thin end of a knife blade that fits into the handle.

→ **Zarf.** Believe it or not, a zarf is a holder for a handleless coffee cup.

➡ **Dingbat.** Dingbat. See those cute little typesetter's marks to the left of each bold-face word in this article? They're dingbats. How about that?

— Reader's Digest

# Synonyms.

A **synonym** is a word that means the same as another. From the list below, choose one of the four words that follow that is most nearly the same in meaning to the word in bold face type.

1. **Incarnate**  a. meat-eater;  b. huckster;  c. personified;  d. rude
2. **Libation**  a. feminist;  b. drink;  c. law suit;  d. liberty
3. **Wily**  a. willful;  b. clever;  c. damp;  d. coyote
4. **Infinite**  a. finished;  b. endless;  c. vague  d. non-believer
5. **Blissful**  a. beatific;  b. smart;  c. bald;  d. dour
6. **Wraith**  a. apparition;  b. anger;  c. decoration;  d. worship
7. **Ephemeral**  a. brilliant;  b. sad;  c. short-lasting;  d. precious
8. **Tenacity**  a. roughness;  b. slum;  c. persistence;  d. tenor
9. **Accolade**  a. liquor;  b. honor;  c. soft drink;  d. instrument
10. **Erudite**  a. airy;  b. scholarly;  c. written;  d. anxiety

# Antonyms

An **antonym** is a word that means the opposite of another. From the list below, choose one of the four words that follow the word in bold face type that is most nearly its opposite.

1. **Appease**  a. anger;  b. please;  c. disappear;  d. jump
2. **Beatitude**  a. altitude;  b. curse;  c. salve;  d. massage
3. **Canine**  a. spiritual;  b. feline;  c. ability;  d.  sparse
4. **Dire**  a. indirect;  b. understood;  c. hopeful;  d. soothing
5. **Florid**  a. pale;  b. wilted;  c. beautiful;  d. ceiling
6. **Gratuitous**  a. clumsy;  b. ungrateful;  c. on purpose;  d. free
7. **Peon**  a. master;  b. dirt;  c. helper;  d. bladder
8. **Rebuff**  a. scratch;  b. polish;  c. embrace;  d. dress
9. **Sequel**  a. preface;  b. disorder;  c. button;  d. epilogue
10. **Tacit**  a. spoken;  b. dull;  c. slippery;  d. remarkable

**For answers, see page 221.**

— John Wester, a friend and fellow teacher.

# Roots.

The English language has approximately 800,000 words. About half of them have their roots in Latin. Over 10% have Greek roots. If you are familiar with the roots, you can grasp the meaning of their many derivatives without having seen them before.

| Latin | Definition | Greek | Definition |
|-------|------------|-------|------------|
| Loqu | Speak | Anthrop | Mankind |
| Ver | Truth | Miso | Hate |
| Corpor | Body | Arch | Rule |
| Tang | Touch | Chron | Time |
| Sag | Wise | Path | Disease |
| Anim | Life | Tom | Cut |
| Mir | Wonder | Psych | Mind |

Study the roots above and see if you can define the words that follow.

| Latin | | Greek | |
|-------|------------|-------|------------|
| **Word** | **Definition** | **Word** | **Definition** |
| 1. Loquacious | | 1. Misanthrope | |
| 2. Verity | | 2. Anarchy | |
| 3. Incorporate | | 3. Chronological | |
| 4. Tangent | | 4. Psychopath | |
| 5. Sage | | 5. Appendectomy | |
| 6. Animate | | | |
| 7. Mirage | | | |

**For answers, see page 221.**

— John Wester

# Word Choice.

In each of the sentences below there is a blank space indicating that a word has been left out. After the sentence are four words. From these four words, choose the one word which, when inserted in the blank space, best fits in with the meaning of the sentence.

1. He _____ his shoulders without speaking.
   a. turned;  b. shrugged;  c. lowered;  d. shed

2. We entered the dining room, where breakfast was _____ .
   a. cooked;  b. found;  c. served;  d. given

3. My blood _____ as I saw a great white shark coming towards me.
   a. boiled;  b. spilled;  c. turned cold;  d. stopped

4. This morning, I was busy _____ in the library.
   a. reading;  b. sleeping;  c. taking a bath;  d. jogging

5. We often saw the hulls of shipwrecked vessels that were rotting in the _____ .
   a. coral;  b. depths;  c. shore;  d. beach

6. I had wished to visit the reef against which the sea, always _____ , broke with great violence.
   a. calm;  b. cold;  c. rough;  d. blue

7. At half-past eight the boat _____ softly aground.
   a. stepped;  b. walked;  c. ran;  d. swam

8. There was no time to _____ .
   a. gain;  b. lose;  c. miss;  d. enjoy

9. They returned to the shore about eleven o'clock _____ the morning.
   a. with;  b. at;  c. for;  d. in

10. For some minutes he was immovable, never taking his _____ from his point of observation.
    a. hand;  b. eye;  c. foot;  d. ear.

For answers, see page 221.

— John Wester

# The Thesaurus.

A **thesaurus** is a book of synonyms designed to help the user find a word to replace another word. A thesaurus can help us find a word that says what we want to express in a better way. Or to express it differently, but meaning the same think. Or a thesaurus can help us find a word that says what we want to say, simply; or find a word so weighted with meaning that it makes us stop and think. Journalists use the thesaurus. Poets use it, too.

In a thesaurus at the end of the lists of synonyms, are antonyms written in bold face type. Below is a game. It consists of a group of synonyms with a word of opposite meaning hidden within the group. See if you can find the one word in each group that means the opposite of the other words.

1. **Substitution**: resemblance, likeness, similitude, semblance, affinity, approximation, inequality, parallelism, agreement, analogy.
2. **Imitation**: emulation, mimicry, mockery, parrotism, echo, simulation, impersonation, masquerade, imagination, plagiarism, forgery, sham, counterfeit, fake.
3. **Forgetfulness**: amnesia, hypomnesia, paramnesia, Lethe, nepenthe, nirvana, amnesty, limbo, oblivion, supersession, repression, memory.
4. **Economy**: management, order, frugality, austerity, prudence, thrift, retrenchment, unselfishness, parsimony.
5. **Discovery**: location, strike, encounter, detection, search, discernment, perception.
6. **Concealment**: obliteration, obscuration, secrecy, privacy, disguise, camouflage, cloak, masquerade, blind, smoke screen, visibility, red herring.
7. **Chance**: accident, fortune, hap, haphazard, hazard, luck, peradventure, possibility, probability, certain, likelihood.
8. **Knowledge**: cognizance, acquaintance, information, ken, learning, erudition, inexperience, wisdom.

**For answers, see page 221.**

— John Wester

# Build your vocabulary,
# learn important beginnings.

**Prefixes** are groups of letters which, when added to the beginning of a word, change its meaning.

## Indicating Direction or Occurrence

| Prefix | Its Meaning | Prefixed Word | Word Meaning |
|---|---|---|---|
| e- | out<br>from | erupt | burst out of |
| ex- | former<br>out | ex-convict<br>expel | former convict<br>force out |
| in- (en-) | not<br>into | inactive<br>ingrown | not active<br>grown into |
| per- | through | perennial | through the year |
| re- | again<br>back | reprint<br>return | print again<br>turn back |
| de- | down<br>away<br>from | descend<br>depart<br>derail | go down<br>go away<br>go from the rail |
| circum- | around | circumnavigate | sail around |
| sub- | lesser<br>under | sub-official<br>submarine | lesser official<br>under water |
| trans- | across | transatlantic | across the Atlantic |
| retro- | back | retroactive | applicable to past events |

— A.R.

# Building a better vocabulary enhances comprehension.

This practice covers **negative prefixes**: non-
dis-
mis-
anti-

Some of the following prefixes have more than one meaning:

| | | |
|---|---|---|
| dishonest | nonexistent | misguide |
| nonpayment | disobedient | antifriction |
| misuse | mistrust | disbelief |
| anticlimax | disagree | mishandle |
| misfortune | nonresistant | nonexplosive |
| nonodorous | misdeed | disinterested |
| disloyal | antifreeze | misjudge |
| misdirect | dislike | antiknock |
| nonsupport | nonsalable | nonbeliever |
| discredit | mispronounce | disown |
| antitrust | discontinue | mismate |
| nonprofit | antisocial | discomfort |
| misunderstood | disorder | disqualify |
| nonconformist | misspell | mislead |
| dissatisfied | nonresident | nonporous |
| misbehave | disapprove | displeasure |

— A.R.

# Vocabulary builders
# – other beginnings.

## Indicating Relationships

| Prefix | Its Meaning | Prefixed Word | Word Meaning |
|---|---|---|---|
| co- | with | coexist | live with |
| com- | | commingle | mingle with |
| con- | | converse | talk with |
| col- | | collaborate | work with |
| cor- | | correlate | relate with |
| counter- | against | countercheck | check against |
| contra- | opposite | contradict | say the opposite |
| hyper- | overly (in excess) | hypersensitive | overly sensitive |
| super- | above | superman | above average man |
| | beyond | supernatural | beyond nature |

## Indicating Time and Number

| Prefix | Its Meaning | Prefixed Word | Word Meaning |
|---|---|---|---|
| pro | on behalf of (prior to) | provide | look ahead |
| pre- | before | preamble | introductory remarks |
| post- | after | postdate | date after |
| uni- | one | uniform | one form |
| bi- | two | biweekly | two times a week |
| tri- | three | tricycle | three wheel |
| hemi- | half | hemisphere | half of a sphere |
| semi | partly | semiconscious | partly conscious |
| multi- | many | multicolored | many colored |

— A.R.

# Answers

## SYNONYMS
(on page 214)

1. c.
2. b.
3. b.
4. b.
5. a.
6. a.
7. c.
8. c.
9. b.
10. b.

## ANTONYMS
(on page 214)

1. a.
2. b.
3. b.
4. c.
5. a.
6. c.
7. a.
8. c.
9. a.
10. a.

## ROOTS
(on page 215)

Latin
1. talkative
2. truth
3. embody
4. touching
5. a wise person
6. to impart life to
7. something illusory

Greek
1. one who hates mankind
2. without rules
3. arrangement in order of occurence
4. mentally ill
5. surgical removal of appendix

## WORD CHOICE
(on page 216)

1. b.
2. c.
3. c.
4. a.
5. b.
6. c.
7. c.
8. b.
9. d.
10. b.

## THE THESAURUS
(on page 217)

1. inequality
2. imagination
3. memory
4. unselfishness
5. search
6. visibility
7. certain
8. inexperience

*"Use the talents you possess,
for the woods would be very silent
if no birds sang except the best."*

**My grandfather would say this
to me when I was a child, to
encourage me when I was ready to
give up on something. Each time,
these words would make me feel
better and I would change my mind
about giving up. I often wonder
where I would be today and what I
would be doing if it were not for
my grandfather's kindness to me.
The lesson in the words is for you,
too, dear reader. Make use of your
abilities, whatever they may be.**

# Bibliography

Allen, D.L. and Mech, L.D., "Wolves Versus Moose on Isle Royale." *National Geographic Magazine,* February 1963.

Asimov, Isaac, *The Human Brain: Its Capacities and Functions.* Boston: Houghton, 1963.

Boorstin, Daniel J., *The Discoverers.* New York: Random House, 1983

Burton, Dr. Maurice, *The International Wildlife Encyclopedia.* New York: Marshall-Cavendish Corporation, 1969.

Caras, Roger, "Like Tin Cats in a Shooting Gallery." *Earth,* November 1971.

Clark, B.H. and Leiber, M., compilers, *Great Short Stories of the World.* New York: Garden City Publishers, 1925.

DeRopp, Robert S., *The Master Game.* New York: Dell Publishing Company, 1968.

Gilbert, Bill, *The Trailblazers.* (Old West Series) New York: Time-Life Books, 1973.

Jung, Carl G., *Flying Saucers, A Modern Myth.* New York: Harcourt, 1959.

———, *Man and His Symbols.* Dell Publishing Company, 1958.

———, *Mandala Symbolism.* Princeton, New Jersey: Princeton University Press, 1959.

Koestler, Arthur, *The Act of Creation.* New York: Dell Publishing Company, 1964.

McCluhan, T.C., *Touch the Earth.* New York: Pocket Books, 1971.

McIntyre, Joan, *Mind in the Waters: a Book to Celebrate the Consciousness of Whales and Dolphins.* New York: Scribner, 1974.

Maltz, Maxwell, *Psycho-cybernetics.* New York: Pocket Books, 1973.

———, *Your Built-in Success Mechanism* (pamphlet) 1960.

Rapaport, David, *Emotions and Memory.* New York: Science Editions, 1961.

Ogburn, Charlton, "What's the Use of Poetry?" *Reader's Digest, December 1982.*

Storm, Hyemeyohsts, *Seven Arrows.* New York: Harper and Row, 1972.

Taylor, John G., *The Shape of Minds to Come.* New York: Weybright and Talley, 1971.

Toffler, Alvin, *Future Shock.* New York: Random House, 1970.

Vietmeyer, Noel D., "Can a Whale Find Life in the Desert?" *Audubon Magazine,* September 1975.

# *Difficulties End With Knowledge*

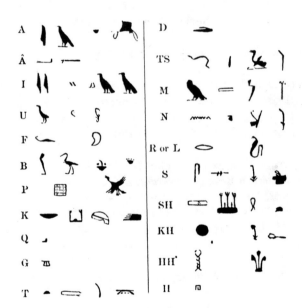

Egyptian hieroglyphics